Constitutional Amendments

Constitutional Amendments

From Freedom of Speech to Flag Burning

Volume 2:
Amendments 9-17

Tom Pendergast, Sara Pendergast, and John Sousanis
Elizabeth Shaw Grunow, Editor

AN IMPRINT OF THE GALE GROUP

DETROIT · NEW YORK · SAN FRANCISCO
LONDON · BOSTON · WOODBRIDGE, CT

Constitutional Amendments
From Freedom of Speech to Flag Burning

Tom Pendergast
Sara Pendergast
John Sousanis

Staff

Elizabeth Shaw Grunow, U·X·L Editor
Carol DeKane Nagel, U·X·L Managing Editor
Thomas L. Romig, U·X·L Publisher

Elizabeth Des Chenes, Richard Clay Hanes, Kris E. Palmer, Contributing Editors

Julie Juengling, Permissions Associate (Pictures)
Robyn Young, Imaging and Multimedia Content Editor
Pamela A. Reed, Imaging Coordinator

Rita Wimberley, Senior Buyer
Evi Seoud, Assistant Manager, Composition Purchasing and Electronic Prepress

Kenn Zorn, Senior Art Director
Pamela A. E. Galbreath, Senior Art Designer

Linda Mahoney, LM Design, Typesetting

Cover photographs: Reproduced by permission of the Library of Congress.

Library of Congress Cataloging-in-Publication Data
Pendergast, Tom.
    Constitutional amendments from freedom of speech to flag burning / Tom Pendergast,
Sara Pendergast, and John Sousanis ; Elizabeth Shaw Grunow, editor.
        p. cm.
    Includes bibliographical references and index.
    ISBN 0-7876-4865-5 (set: hardcover)-ISBN 0-7876-4866-3 (v.1)-ISBN 0-7876-4867-1
(v.2)-ISBN 0-7876-4868-X (v.3)
        1.Constitutional amendments-United States-Juvenile literature. 2. Constitutional
law-United States-Juvenile literature. 3. Civil rights-United States-Juvenile literature.
[1. Constitutional amendments. 2. Constitutional law. 3. Civil rights.] I. Title:
Constitutional amendments. II. Pendergast, Sara. III. Sousanis, John. IV. Title.

KF4557 .P46 2001
342.73'03-dc21

00-067236

Printed in the United States of America

10 9 8 7 6 5

Contents

Volume 1

Contents

Reader's Guide

The Constitution of the United States has been the supreme law of the land for more than two centuries, since it was formally adopted in 1788. The Constitution's longevity as the basis for the U.S. government owes much to its original framers. Their decision to provide a system of checks and balances among the various branches of government and to create a form of representation that took into account the interests of big and small states left room for a growing country to adapt and reinterpret the Constitution. However, the Constitution has never been a purely static document: because the framers created a process for amending the Constitution, over the years the document has been changed and expanded in response to changes in American society. It is a process that is never taken lightly, for it means tinkering with the very framework of the nation's political system. Yet from the years immediately following its ratification through the 1990s, Americans have successfully amended the Constitution twenty-seven times, and made attempts to change it numerous other times.

Constitutional Amendments: From Freedom of Speech to Flag Burning devotes a single chapter to each of the existing amendments to the United States Constitution as well as a final chapter that looks at several amendment proposals that have not been ratified.

An Introduction provides general information about the drafting of the Constitution, the interpretive powers of the Supreme Court, and the ratification process that supplements the information provided for each of the individual amendments.

Chapters average approximately six thousand words in length and examine the historical origins of the amendment, the drafting and ratification of the amendment, and the consequent impact the amendment has had on American society. In general, cases pertaining to an amendment are discussed in chronological order. However, in some instances an amendment's various clauses are discussed separately in order to clarify the particular significance of each clause.

Additional Features

Constitutional Amendments is organized for easy fact-finding:

- Each chapter is headed by the full text of the constitutional amendment it is covering.

- Standard sidebars containing the ratification facts of each amendment also appear at the beginning of each chapter.

- The issues and amendments are presented in language accessible to middle school users.

- Challenging terms are sometimes used, so a Words to Know section is included in each volume. The section defines words and terms used in the set that may be unfamiliar to students.

- Sources for further study are included at the end of each chapter.

- The three volumes also contain more than 150 photos and illustrations to further enhance the text.

- Each of the three volumes also includes a research topics section and a general subject index for locating key people, places, events, and cases discussed throughout *Constitutional Amendments.*

Suggestions Are Welcome

We welcome your comments on *Constitutional Amendments: From Freedom of Speech to Flag Burning.* Please write, Editors, *Constitutional Amendments,* U•X•L, 27500 Drake Road, Farmington Hills, MI 48331-3535; call toll-free: 1-800-877-4253; fax to 248-414-5043; or send e-mail via http://www.galegroup.com.

Advisory Board

Special thanks are due for the invaluable comments and suggestions provided by U•X•L's *Constitutional Amendments advisors:*

- Connie Altimore, American History teacher, Northeast Middle School, Midland, Michigan
- Nancy Guidry, Young Adult Librarian, Santa Monica Public Library, Santa Monica, California
- Ann Marie LaPrise, Children's Librarian and Assistant Manager, Elmwood Park Branch, Detroit Public Library, Detroit, Michigan

Contributors

The following writers contributed to U•X•L's *Constitutional Amendments:*

- John Sousanis, chapters 1-10, 12
- Tina Gianoulis, chapters 11, 16, 24, 27
- Richard Clay Hanes, chapters 13-15
- Sara Pendergast, chapters 17, 25
- Tom Pendergast, chapters 18, 21, 22, 23 (with Tim Seul), 28
- Tim Seul, chapters 19, 20, 23 (with Tom Pendergast), 26

Research and Activity Ideas

The following list of research and activity ideas is intended to offer suggestions for complementing social studies and history curricula, to trigger additional ideas for enhancing learning, and to suggest cross-disciplinary projects for library and classroom use.

Discussing a Free Press: The First Amendment limits government interference with a free press. Consider how the news media might differ if the government were allowed to directly influence or censor the press. Make a list of all the stories in a single edition of a newspaper or weekly news magazine. Have students discuss which stories might be censored if the First Amendment didn't exist. Physically cut these stories from the publication to demonstrate the impact the Amendment has had. For further discussion, have students suggest stories that a government-controlled press might add to a newspaper, such as articles praising officials or government actions. Finally, discuss the impact a government-controlled press might have on today's society.

Religious Diversity: The First Amendment's Establishment Clause helps protect religious diversity in the United States. Using almanacs, census data, or other sources, create graphs and charts that compare how many different religions are practiced in your community, your county, and your state. Discuss how life might be different if there were a single government-established religion.

Debating the Right to Bear Arms: Over the years the Second Amendment has been interpreted quite differently by different groups. Groups debate whether the amendment simply protects a

Research and Activity Ideas

state's right to establish a militia or whether it also guarantees the individual's right to own weapons. After discussing the chapter on the Second Amendment divide the class in half, with each half taking one side of the debate. The students in each group should work together to rewrite the amendment in a way they believe clearly states their side of the debate. Then have the entire class discuss how the proposed amendments would affect today's society.

Living the Third Amendment: The Third Amendment limits the practice of quartering (or housing) soldiers in private homes. During the French and Indian War, American colonist were sometimes forced to house British soldiers in their homes. Imagine that your family has been asked to house one or more soldiers. Write a journal entry discussing how such an arrangement might impact your daily life.

Voting Rights: The Fifteenth, Nineteenth and Twenty-sixth Amendments granted the right to vote to groups of people who were previously denied the right. To help students understand the importance of political participation, divide the class into groups by gender, birth months, or other criteria. Then put several fictitious decisions up for a vote, such as which popular band the class would like to invite to play at the school or which team sport should be cut from the school's athletic program. With each vote, look at how the results would differ if one or another group's votes were not counted. Discuss the impact of limiting or widening the number of people allowed to vote in real elections.

Government Bans: Look at the history of the temperance (anti-alcohol) movement. Discuss why the Eighteenth Amendment prohibition on alcohol sales and consumption was passed and the reasons the Twenty-first Amendment later repealed it. Consider the difficulties of establishing a complete ban on other products considered unhealthy or dangerous, such as cigarettes.

Interpreting Amendments: Over the years the Supreme Court has changed the way it interprets various Constitutional amendments. Track the Court's changing interpretation of a particular amendment from the time it was passed to the present day. Discuss how the same amendment could be understood differently at different times in history and by different justices.

Draft a New Amendment: Divide your class into groups and have each group choose an issue they feel strongly about. Have the group write a proposal for a constitutional amendment that incorporates their idea. Issues could range from serious political issues to more frivolous ideas such as imposing a national dress code. Each group should then present its amendment for debate with the rest of the class. Discuss whether the amendments might be interpreted to mean something other than what the drafters intended. After the class discussion, allow each group to rewrite their amendment. Finally, put the redrafted amendments up for a vote of the class.

Unratified Amendments: Chapter twenty-eight looks at a number of unratified constitutional amendments. Have students write an essay on how American society might be different if one of these amendments were ratified.

Words to Know

A

Abolition: Total opposition to all slavery.

Abolitionists: Those who fought for an end to slavery.

Abortion: A biological event or medical procedure that terminates a pregnancy.

Abridge: To lessen.

Absentee ballot: A ballot that can be mailed in, so that a person can vote if they are away from home during an election.

Abstinence: The act of abstaining or avoiding something, for instance, the use of alcoholic beverages.

Acquittal: A trial outcome in which a defendant is free from a charge.

Activist: Someone who works hard for a political cause.

Aerial surveillance: Watching activity from the air, usually in a helicopter or airplane.

Affirmation: A solemn declaration.

Appeal: A legal proceeding in which a case is taken before a higher court for rehearing.

Apportionment: The process of determining how many representatives a particular state, county, or other kind of region should send to a legislature.

Articles of Confederation: An early constitution for the United States that set up a weak central government. The document was ratified in 1781 but was replaced by the U.S. Constitution in 1789.

Assistance of counsel: The help of outsiders in a trial. The term usually applies to the aid of a professional attorney.

Attorney: A person who is legally qualified to represent someone or some group in a court of law. A lawyer.

B

Billet: Lodging for troops in nonmilitary buildings.

Bill of Rights: The first ten amendments to the U.S. Constitution. These amendments clarify certain personal freedoms not clearly defined in the language of the Constitution.

Bipartisan: Supported by two groups/political parties.

Bond: A certificate issued by a company or government that promises to pay back the cost of the certificate with interest.

Bootlegging: The illegal manufacture, sale, or transportation of liquor.

Bounty: A reward for performing a certain task.

Boycott: A political tactic by which a group of people refuse to use a product or service to protest something they don't like about the producers of the product or service.

British Empire: Worldwide territories governed by or linked to Great Britain.

C

Candidate: A person nominated for a political office.

Capital crime: A crime that is punishable by death.

Capital gains: The profit that is made from selling something.

Civil rights: A series of basic rights written in the Constitution and identified through time that are to be enjoyed by all citizens without undue government interference.

Civil trial: A trial in which a person (or group) who has been injured seeks payment from the person who caused the injury. In a civil trial the person bringing the case to the court is seeking a remedy (solution) to a problem, whereas in a criminal trial an entity (usually the state) is seeking to have someone punished for an illegal action.

Civil War: War fought between the Northern (Union) states and the Southern (Confederate) states from 1861 to1865 over issues such as state and federal power and the future of slavery in the United States.

Coalition: A temporary alliance of different groups seeking a similar goal.

Cold War: A state of political tension between the Soviet Union and the United States that lasted from roughly 1947 to 1989.

Colony: A territory controlled by a distant government.

Commerce: The large-scale exchange of goods and products involving transportation.

Common law: Legal tradition. Many of America's legal traditions can be traced to English common law.

Compensation: Something given to someone in return for something else; often, payment given in exchange for work performed.

Compromise of 1850: A political deal aimed at easing the conflict between slave and free states, this compromise allowed California to join the United States as a free state in exchange for giving slave owners the right to travel into free territory to capture runaway slaves.

Compulsory process: A process by which courts subpoena (command someone to appear in court) witnesses for the defense and prosecution.

Confederacy: Also known as the Confederate States of America; the eleven Southern states that seceded, or withdrew, from the United States during the Civil War (1861–65).

Congress: The legislative, or law making, branch of the U.S. government. Congress is made up of two parts, called houses: the Senate and the House of Representatives. The Senate gives each state equal representation, while representation in the House of Representatives is roughly proportionate to the state's share of the country's total population.

Words to Know

Conscription: Compulsory enrollment in the armed forces; the draft.

Consensus: Widespread agreement; an opinion reached by the majority.

Construe: To interpret.

Consumer: Someone who uses or buys a product or service.

Conviction: A trial outcome in which a defendant is found guilty of a charge.

Corruption: Wrong-doing in government.

Criminal trial: A trial in which the government seeks to punish someone for a crime. In a criminal trial an entity (usually the state) is seeking to have someone punished for an illegal action, whereas in a civil trial the person bringing the case to the court is seeking a remedy (solution) to a problem.

D

Declaration of Independence: Completed on July 4, 1776, the document—which was written primarily by Thomas Jefferson—lists the complaints of the thirteen American colonies against Great Britain and formally announces their independence from the British Empire.

Deduction: In taxes, an expense a taxpayer can subtract from his/her taxable income.

Desecration: The violation of something sacred.

Discrimination: Giving privileges to one group but not to another similar group.

Diplomat: Someone who represents the government of his or her country during relations with other countries.

Direct election: An election in which people vote, not an election in which representatives vote in the place of the public.

Domestic product: Something that is made within a country. The opposite of domestic is foreign.

Due process: Proceedings carried out within established guidelines that do not limit or violate a person's legal rights.

E

Effective counsel: Helpful legal assistance.

Electors: Representatives from each state who cast the actual votes for president and vice president of the United States.

Electoral College: A body of electors, or representatives, from each state, who elect the president and vice president of the United States. These electors vote based on numbers gathered through the count of the popular vote in each state, which is the actual vote of the citizens of that state.

Electoral majority: Votes from a majority of the electors in the Electoral College.

Emancipation: The act of freeing one person from the control and authority of another.

Embargo: A government order forbidding trade with another country.

Eminent domain: Literally, the term means "highest claim to ownership of land." The concept allows a government to take private property for public use because the government is thought to have eminent domain over all the lands it rules.

Enumerated rights: Rights that are specifically defined in the Constitution or its amendments.

Enumeration: An official count, as of the number of citizens in a legislative district.

E pluribus unum: A Latin phrase meaning "Out of many, one." It is one of the mottoes of the United States.

Equal protection of the laws: A right that states that no person or class of persons can be denied the same protection of the laws pertaining to their lives, property, and pursuit of happiness as others in similar circumstances.

Equitable claim: A civil claim in which the plaintiff (person bringing suit in court) seeks to cause the defendant to perform certain actions (or to stop performing others). Equitable claims are not covered by the Seventh Amendment.

Ethics: Moral values.

Words to Know

Evangelical: Characterized by ardent or crusading enthusiasm. Evangelical churches actively seek to spread their message and recruit new members.

Exclusionary rule: A legal concept asserting that evidence found during an illegal search should not be used against a defendant in court. The exclusionary rule is a relatively recent concept in legal history that is now applied in most American criminal trials.

Excise tax: An extra charge added to the price of some domestic products.

Exemption: In taxes, part of the income on which the taxpayer is allowed not to pay taxes.

Express powers: Federal powers that are specifically enumerated or listed in the Constitution or its amendments.

F

Faithless elector: A term used to describe a representative who does not vote the way he or she had promised to before being selected to the Electoral College. By the end of the twentieth century, only eight electors in the history of the Electoral College had cast such "faithless" votes.

Farmer's alliances: Groups of farmers who met to discuss their problems and agree on common goals so that they could increase their political power and improve the conditions of their lives.

Federalism: The type of government in which separate states come together to form a union. Also, the kind of politics within such a government by which people believe the states should have their own identity and power separate from the national government.

Federalist Party: A political party founded in 1787 that argued for the establishment of a strong federal (central or national) government.

Federation: A government in which separate states unite for greater strength.

Filibuster: An attempt to obstruct the passage of legislation, often with prolonged speechmaking.

Flat tax: A tax with one rate for everyone.

Flogging: Very hard beating, usually with a whip or a stick.

Frisk: To search a person by running ones hand over the person's clothes and through his or her pockets.

Fruit from the poisonous tree: A term for evidence that is obtained as a direct result of other illegally obtained evidence. Such "fruit" is often not allowed to be used in court.

G

General warrant: A type of warrant (a document issued by a judge allowing the holder to search the premises) used by British officials until the end of the eighteenth century. A general warrant lacked probable cause and usually did not name specific people or places to be searched.

Good faith exception: A concept that allows illegally gained evidence to be used in court, if the police officer did not willfully break the law in obtaining it. Allows for honest mistakes by law enforcement officials.

Graduated tax: A tax where the rate increases in steps, little by little.

Grand jury: A group of citizens assembled to decide if the government has enough evidence against an accused person to justify holding a trial.

Great Britain: At the time of the American Revolution, Great Britain was a single state made up of England, Wales, and Scotland. Today, Great Britain, or the United Kingdom, also includes Northern Ireland. Great Britain ruled the thirteen American colonies until the American Revolution in 1776.

Great Depression: A worldwide economic collapse that began with the stock market crash of 1929.

Grievance: A complaint about an unjust act.

H

Historical test: The method used to determine which civil cases are entitled to a jury trial under the Seventh Amendment. If a case in federal courts historically would have been entitled to a jury trial under English common law, a jury is used.

House of Representatives: The lower house in Congress. Each state's representation in the house is roughly proportionate to its share of the total population. Every state has at least one representative.

I

Immunity: Exemption (to be excused) from regular legal requirements and penalties.

Impeachment: The process by which an elected official is removed from office.

Implied powers: Federal powers that are only hinted at or suggested by the Constitution.

Inauguration: The ceremony by which newly elected presidents and vice presidents are sworn into office.

Income: Money earned from working, investing, renting, or selling things.

Incriminate: To accuse or blame someone for a crime.

Indictment: A formal charge prepared by the government against a defendant that is agreed to by a grand jury or by a judge in a hearing.

Informant: A person who gives information or tips to law enforcement officers.

Insurrection: Rising up against established authority.

Integration: To bring together or blend; commonly used to describe a mixture of different races of people.

Internal Revenue Code (U.S. Tax Code): The collection of all the laws and rules that concern federal income tax.

Intervene: To come between.

Involuntary servitude: The state in which a person works for another person against his or her will due to force, imprisonment, or coercion, regardless of whether the person is being paid for their labor.

J

Jeopardy: Exposure to danger of death, loss, or injury. The type of danger a defendant is in while on trial for a criminal offense.

Jim Crow: Legally enforced racial segregation, named after a stereotypical black character in a minstrel show.

Jurisdiction: The power and authority to interpret and apply the law. A court has jurisdiction in a district, or defined area.

Just compensation: A fair payment for losses.

L

Lame duck: A name given to an elected official continuing in office during the period between a failed election bid and the inauguration of a successor. "Lame duck" politicians are thought to be ineffective and without power.

Legislature: An official law-making governmental body or assembly.

Literacy test: A test a voter had to pass before being able to vote in an election. The tests were considered controversial because they prevented those who were denied equal access to an education the right to vote.

Lynch: To execute someone without due process of law, often by hanging.

M

Magistrate: A judge or other court official capable of issuing a warrant.

Magna Carta: A document, signed by King John I of England in 1215, outlining personal and political freedoms granted to English citizens.

Majority: More than half of a total.

Mandate: A show of support by voters for their elected representative. A president is thought to have a mandate to enact his proposals when he receives broad popular support.

Maritime: Relating to navigation or commerce on the seas.

Miranda warnings: Standard warnings about rights and responsibilities that are read or spoken to a suspect in police custody before he or she is interrogated. The Supreme Court established the warnings in the case of *Miranda v. Arizona* (1966).

Missouri Compromise: A political deal aimed at easing the conflict between slave and free states, this 1820 compromise drew a line across lands acquired in the Louisiana Purchase and declared that states admitted south of the line could allow slave holding but that states north of the line must be free.

Muckraking: Journalism that exposes corruption in public life.

N

Narrow interpretation: To greatly limit the meaning of something.

Naturalization: A process in which a person may gain citizenship by meeting certain requirements such as length of residence or act of Congress.

Nationalism: Within a federation, it is the political belief that the national government should be more powerful than the state governments.

Negotiate: To settle disagreements or resolve issues by discussion and mutual agreement.

Nominate: To appoint or propose a candidate for office.

P

Pacifist: Someone who believes that war or violence is the wrong way to settle disputes.

Parliament: Great Britain's legislative (law-making) assembly.

Particularity requirement: One of the conditions a warrant must meet to be deemed legal under the Fourth Amendment. To meet the particularity requirement, the warrant must list the particular people and places to be searched and the specific kinds of evidence that an officer hopes to obtain.

Party: Group of people organized with the purpose of directing government policies.

Patent: An official government grant giving someone the right to be the only one to make a product or perform a process that he or she invented for a certain period of time.

Patent law: Laws dealing with the ownership of new inventions and commercial processes.

Pensions: Regular payments of money other than for salary, such as for retirement or disability.

Peonage: Forcing a person against his or her will to work for another to pay a debt.

Per diem: Latin, meaning "per day;" the rate of payment a person receives per day.

Plaintiff: The party who sues in a civil action; a complainant; the prosecution—that is, a state or the United States representing the people—in a criminal case.

Plain view rule: A rule that allows officers to seize evidence they do not have a warrant for if they come across the evidence legally.

Plurality: In an election among three or more candidates, a number of votes cast for one candidate that is greater than the number cast for any other candidate, but that is still less than half of the total number of votes.

Plutocrat: A wealthy person with the power to influence government. A plutocracy is a government ruled by a wealthy class.

Police power: A recognized general legal authority not specifically mentioned in the U.S. Constitution that states hold to govern their citizens, lands, or natural resources.

Political appointment: A job within the government that is filled by a person chosen by an elected official.

Poll: A survey by which a random group of people are asked their opinions in order to predict how most people feel about a subject. The Gallup Poll is a respected and famous polling company.

Poll taxes: Fees charged to citizens to vote at the voting (polling) place.

Popular majority: More than half of the votes case by the voting public.

Popular vote: In the U.S. presidential election process, the votes cast by the public rather than by the Electoral College.

Precedent: An instance that serves as an example for dealing with similar situations.

President: The highest elected office in U.S. government. The leader of the executive branch of government.

Words to Know

Presidential disability: The inability of the President to function in office.

President Pro Tempore: Senator who presides over the Senate in the absence of the vice president. Also considered the Senate's presiding officer, the president pro tempore is included in the line of succession should the offices of the president and vice president become vacant.

Probable cause: Information that would lead a reasonable person to believe that an officer's request for a warrant is merited.

Procedural due process: The constitutional guarantee that one's liberty and property rights may not be affected unless reasonable notice and an opportunity to be heard in order to present a claim or defense are provided.

Progressive era: A period from roughly 1900 to 1920 during which many Americans supported the improvement of society through changes in government and social policy.

Progressive tax: A tax that is based upon a person's ability to pay; the more a person earns or has, the more he or she pays in tax.

Prohibition: A period from 1920 to 1933 when the Eighteenth Amendment to the Constitution made the manufacture, sale, or transportation of intoxicating liquors within the United States illegal.

Prosecute: To begin civil or criminal legal proceedings.

Prosecutor: The government attorney in a criminal case.

Public rights: Rights created by Congress that were not in existence at the time the Bill of Rights was adopted. These rights are not subject to the traditions of common law.

R

Radical: Extreme. A radical change is a complete change; a person who is a radical advocates complete change of a system.

Ratification: A process in which three-fourths of the states must approve proposed amendments to the Constitution before the amendment can become formally adopted.

Reasonable expectation of privacy: One of the standards used to determine if a warrant is required to gather evidence. If a person has good reason to expect privacy (such as in their home or their car) a warrant is usually required before searching is permitted.

Redcoat: Slang term for British soldiers that refers to their bright red uniform jackets.

Regressive tax: A tax by which everyone is charged the same rate of tax, no matter how much property or income they may have.

Repeal: To revoke or rescind an official act or law. In the United States the repeal movement was directed to revoking the Eighteenth Amendment; it succeeded in 1933 with the passage of the Twenty-first Amendment.

Republic: A form of government in which government officials are elected by voters.

Retroactive: Something that applies to time already past.

Revenue: The income of a government.

S

Scandal: An embarrassing or dishonest action that offends the public and damages someone's reputation.

Secede: To break away from an organization.

Second Great Awakening: A period between roughly 1820 and 1850 when religious enthusiasm swept the country and church attendance grew dramatically.

Segregation: Keeping racial groups from mixing, such as maintaining separate facilities for members of different races or restricting use of facilities to members of one race.

Seizure: The forcible taking of property or other evidence.

Senate: The upper house of Congress. Two senators represent each state equally in the Senate.

Servitude: Owning another person who performs duties.

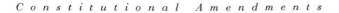

Silver platter doctrine: A court ruling that allowed federal officials to use illegally gathered evidence if it were presented to them by state law enforcement officials on "a silver platter." The doctrine was eliminated in 1960.

Slavery: The owning of other persons to perform work.

Sobriety: Moderation or abstinence in the consumption of alcoholic beverages.

Sovereign: The government body or person with supreme authority, such as the president, or a king or queen.

Sovereign immunity: The concept under common law by which the government is protected against any lawsuit by its people. Under certain circumstances, the government may choose to waive this right and allow people to take legal action against it or its agents.

Sovereignty: Controlling body of power or government authority.

Speakeasy: Any place in which people may buy or consume illegal alcoholic beverages.

Speaker of the House of Representatives: The U.S. representative selected to lead the House of Representatives.

Spoils system: A system for making appointments to public office based on how well appointees had served the party in power. The spoils system was often used in the nineteenth century.

State government: The government of an individual state. The Tenth Amendment grants state governments all government power that is not granted to the federal government by the Constitution.

Statesman: Someone who is skilled at the business of government or politics.

Subsidy: Money given by the government to help individuals or businesses.

Substantive due process: The concept that there are certain essential rights that no law can take away.

Subpoena: A court order commanding a person to appear in court.

Succession: The order in which designated people assume a title of office (for example, the presidency).

Suffrage: The right to vote at public elections.

Suffragist: Supporters of a woman's right to vote.

Sumptuary laws: Laws that regulate personal behavior on moral or religious grounds. Opponents of the Eighteenth Amendment complained that it was a sumptuary law.

Supreme Court: The highest court in the United States. Considered the final interpreter of American law.

Supreme Court justice: A judge who serves on the Supreme Court.

T

"Take the fifth": A phrase used to indicate that a person is using their Fifth Amendment protection against self-incrimination.

Tariff: An extra charge added onto the price of an imported product.

Tax bracket: A range of income that is taxed at a certain rate.

Tax evasion: Purposely not paying one's income tax.

Teetotaler: Someone who abstains from drinking any alcohol.

Temperance: A philosophy of moderation or abstinence, especially with regard to alcoholic beverages. The Temperance movement in the United States led to the passage of the Eighteenth Amendment, prohibiting the sale or manufacture of alcohol, in 1919.

Tenure: Length of time in a position or office.

Ticket: A list of candidates for nomination or election.

Tithing: Voluntarily giving a percentage of one's income—most often ten percent—usually to a religious group.

U

Unanimous verdict: A verdict to which all members of a jury agree to.

Unenumerated rights: Rights that exist despite the fact that they are not mentioned or listed in the Constitution.

Union: Name given to the states that did not secede, or withdraw, from the United States during the Civil War (1861–65). The term also refers to a group of workers who unite in order to bargain (set wages and working conditions) with their employer.

Unit rule: A rule that gives all of a state's electoral votes to representatives of the party that wins the popular vote in that state.

V

Valid: Having legal authority or force.

Verdict: The formal decision or finding made by a jury concerning the questions submitted to it during a trial. The jury reports the verdict to the court, which generally accepts it.

Vice president: The second highest elected office in U.S. government. The vice president serves as the president of the Senate and also serves as president if the president is unable to do so.

W

Waive: To willingly give up a right, title, or something that is rightfully due to you.

Warrant: A document issued by a judge allowing the holder to search the premises.

Whig Party: A political party of the nineteenth century that was formed to oppose the Democratic Party. The Whigs encouraged the loose interpretation of the Constitution.

Wiretap: Any electronic device that allows eavesdropping on phone conversations.

Writs of assistance: A form of warrant once used by British officials in the American colonies. The general warrant allowed nearly unlimited searches and seizures of property.

Wrong-winner argument: An argument that states that, under certain circumstances, the Electoral College system in the United States could elect a president that was not, in fact, the people's choice.

Introduction: The Constitution and the Amendment Process

The United States Constitution and its twenty-seven amendments comprise the supreme law of the United States of America. Together they create the structure of American government: granting powers to the branches of government while simultaneously imposing strict limits on those powers. Although written more than two centuries ago, the Constitution has proven able to adapt to the changes in American society—while also helping to shape many of those changes. The ratified constitutional amendments altered aspects of the way Americans govern themselves, and most have had a lasting legal and cultural impact.

A New Nation is Born

In the years before the American Revolutionary War (1775–83) the thirteen original states were individual colonies governed by the British government. The men and women who lived in these territories tended to identify themselves as citizens of the individual colonies (such as Virginians or New Yorkers) rather than as part of a larger America.

In the early 1700s, the colonists found themselves increasingly at odds with the British government over issues such as taxation, tariffs, and the increased presence of the British Army in the colonies (see chapter three). There was a growing feeling within the colonies that Great Britain was infringing upon individual liberties (freedoms). Citizens of the various colonies began to band together in opposition to British rule.

Introduction

As political tension grew within the colonies, military tension grew between the colonial militias (bands of citizen soldiers) and British troops. The first battle of the American Revolution broke out in the spring of 1775. On July 4, 1776, the colonies signed the Declaration of Independence, formally calling for an end to the colonies' political connection to Great Britain. After six years of fighting, the colonies' Continental Army won the last battle of the American Revolutionary War in 1781. The superior leadership of General George Washington (1732–1799) led the colonies to their independence. He eventually became the first president of the United States.

Surprisingly enough, after their successful military cooperation, the thirteen states found that they now valued their independence not only from Great Britain, but also from one another.

The Articles of Confederation: A "league of friendship"

Not surprisingly, when the newly liberated states agreed to form a central government under a document known as the Articles of Confederation and Perpetual Union (commonly referred to as the Articles of Confederation), the government they set up had very little power of its own.

The Articles had originally been drafted in 1776, but were revised and approved by representatives of the thirteen colonies in November 1777. The original proposal was supposed to have created a powerful central government, but by the time the articles were ratified (agreed to) by several states in 1781, the document had been changed dramatically.

Under the Articles of Confederation, the federal (central or national) government was "a firm league of friendship" between the states. The Continental Congress, set up by the Articles of Confederation, was made up of a single assembly (or house) in which each state had only one vote. Nine of the thirteen votes were needed to pass any significant laws, and a unanimous vote was required to change the Articles. There also was no president under the Articles of Confederation, and the national courts were given legal power over very few cases.

SHAYS' REBELLION. The government under the Articles of Confederation was too weak to levy and collect taxes and could neither pay the country's debts nor defend the nation's borders. But it was a military uprising led by Massachusetts farmers that called many politicians' attention to the government's limitations. A severe depression (economic downturn) in the 1780s caused hundreds of farmers to lose their homes and land to debt. In what became known as Shays' Rebellion, several hundred farmers in Massachusetts banded together to protest the farmers' plights. Led by Daniel Shays, a former captain in the Continental Army, the farmers took over courthouses in five counties in the summer and fall of 1786.

Then in January 1787, the farmers marched on federal troops in Springfield, Massachusetts. After ten days of fighting, the federal troops put down the rebellion. But the battle convinced many political leaders that America's central government had to be strengthened. Shortly after Shays' Rebellion, the Continental Congress invited delegates from the states to a convention in Philadelphia, Pennsylvania, to revise the Articles of Confederation.

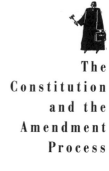

The Philadelphia Convention: Crafting a Stronger Government

The Philadelphia Convention began in May 1787. Interestingly, although the conventioneers were supposed to be working out a plan for strengthening the national government, the convention ended up being divided between Federalists, who favored a stronger central government, and Anti-Federalists, who opposed giving the central government any more power than it already had.

Several prominent Federalists such as James Madison (1751–1836) and Virginia governor Edmund Randolph (1753–1813) were among the first delegates to arrive in Philadelphia. They quickly drafted the so-called "Virginia Plan," which proposed scrapping the Articles of Confederation altogether to create a strong central government consisting of "supreme Legislative, Executive, and Judiciary" branches. The first delegates to attend the convention quickly adopted the Virginia Plan.

As more delegates arrived at the convention, however, the number of Anti-Federalists in attendance grew. The Anti-Federalists believed that the Articles of Confederation needed only a few amendments to make the existing government as effective as it needed to be. The Anti-Federalists plan, known as the "New Jersey Plan," called for giving the central government far less power than the Virginia Plan did.

As each article of the already adopted Virginia Plan was debated at the convention, the Anti-Federalists chipped away at the plan, until the two sides arrived at system of government that represented a compromise between the Federalists and the Anti-Federalists.

Introduction

The Constitution of the United States.

Reproduced by permission of Archive Photos, Inc.

The Constitution of the United States: A Delicate Balancing Act

Although the new Constitution called for a strong central government, the states also retained a great deal of power. This system of "dual sovereignty" (two powers) allowed both governments to exist at once.

The Constitution created at the Philadelphia convention gave the central government specific powers. The states, on the other hand, were to retain any government powers they already had had that were not specifically granted to the central government. This division of power between the central government and the state governments, known as the federal system of government, remains in place to this day.

The central government under the Constitution is divided into three branches: legislative, executive, and judicial. The legislative (lawmaking) branch of government is the Congress. The executive branch is led by the President, and is responsible for enforcing federal laws and carrying out national policies. The judicial branch, the national court system headed by the Supreme Court, is responsible for cases arising from federal and constitutional laws.

Each branch of government is granted specific areas of responsibility, but the Constitution also gives each branch some oversight of the others. This system of "checks and balances" between the branches of government is intended to prevent any branch from becoming too powerful.

Congress: The two-house compromise

The self-interests of the various states at the convention led to the formation of a unique legislative body. Large states argued that the number of representatives each state sent to the legislature (Congress) should be based on the states' population (how many people lived in each state). Southern states, which had large populations of slaves at the time, argued that they should be able to count the slaves when determining how many representatives they sent to Congress. Delegates from smaller states argued for equal representation for every state, regardless of its population. Delegates from the northern states, where slavery was far less common, however, opposed the use of slaves in determining representation.

The convention eventually reached a compromise, creating a Congress made up of two houses, or assemblies. In the upper house of Congress—the Senate—each state would be represented by two senators, giving the states equal standing. However, in the lower house of Congress—the House of Representatives—a state's representation would be determined by the relative size of its population (the larger a state's population, the more representatives that state sent to the House of Representatives). Bills (proposed laws) must be passed by both houses before they could become law.

Additionally, the Convention agreed that a state's population would be determined by counting the number of free persons (non-slaves) in the state and adding "three-fifths of all other Persons" [slaves] while "excluding Indians," who neither voted nor were taxed. (Slavery was abolished altogether in 1865 by the Thirteenth Amendment [see chapter thirteen]).

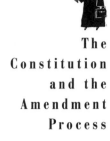

Introduction

Article I, section 8 of the Constitution outlines most of the powers granted to Congress. These include the power to impose taxes, to provide for the common defense and general welfare of the United States, and to regulate commerce. Congress was also empowered to create a national currency (money), a postal system, and a system of courts below the Supreme Court. Only Congress can declare war and is given the power to raise and support an army and navy. More generally, the Constitution's "necessary and proper" clause states that Congress has the power "to make all laws which shall be necessary and proper for carrying into execution

The president oversees many different aspects of running the country. Reproduced by permission of AP/Wide World Photos.

the foregoing powers, and all other powers vested by the Constitution in the government of the United States."

The Executive Branch: All the president's men

Under Article II of the Constitution, the president holds executive (or administrative) power. Presidents are elected to a four-year term by an Electoral College, made up of electors chosen by each of the states (see chapter twelve).

The president is the commander-in-chief of the nation's armed forces, and is responsible for ensuring that federal laws are "faithfully executed," which gives the president control over federal law enforcement agencies. The president also is responsible for appointing judges and federal officials and has the power to negotiate treaties (agreements) with other nations.

The vice president serves as president of the Senate and casts the deciding vote in any tie votes in that house. The vice president has few other powers, but must step in for the president if the president is unable to perform the executive duties.

The Judicial Branch: Supreme powers

Article III of the Constitution establishes the Supreme Court as the highest court in the United States. Congress may also create any lower courts it deems necessary. Federal judges are appointed for life, so that they will be less likely to give in to political pressure when deciding cases.

Federal courts hear cases arising from federal laws, or cases in which the federal government is involved, or where citizens from two different states are involved. The Supreme Court, however, generally hears cases only on appeal, that is, when a party in the case requests that the Court reconsider the ruling of a lower court. The Supreme Court's decisions cannot be appealed, and the Court serves as the final interpreter

The Supreme Court in 1868. Reproduced by permission of the Corbis Corporation (Bellevue).

of the laws of the United States, including all matters dealing with the Constitution and its amendments.

The Court consisted of six justices (judges) until 1869, when it was officially expanded to nine justices. In deciding cases, justices may write individual opinions (written explanations of the justice's reasoning in a case) or sign another justice's opinion. Regardless of how many opinions the Court issues in a case, its final ruling is decided by a simple vote of the justices.

Because it is the final interpreter of law in the United States, the Supreme Court has played a significant role in the history of the Constitution's various amendments.

Checks and balances: The branches' overlapping powers

As stated above, each of the three branches of government exercises some oversight of the others. The Senate must approve all treaties negotiated by the executive branch. While the president is commander-in-chief of the armed forces, only Congress can declare war. The president, on the other hand, may veto (reject) any bill passed by Congress. Once vetoed, a two-thirds majority in both houses of Congress must pass a bill for it to become law.

While the president appoints all federal judges and government officers, the Senate must also approve those appointments. Furthermore, the House of Representatives has the power to impeach (officially accuse of legal misconduct) judges and government officials. Once impeached, these officials (including the president) may be tried in the Senate, and if convicted may be removed from office.

Finally, the Supreme Court may use its power to interpret laws and the Constitution to strike down any laws or government actions it deems illegal or unconstitutional.

Ratifying the Constitution: A Question of Rights

Despite the Constitution's federal system of state and central government, and the system of checks and balances, many delegates to the Constitutional Convention worried that the new government would become too powerful. Toward the end of the convention, a debate began over whether the Constitution should include a bill of rights (a specific list of the people's rights).

James Madison drafted the original amendments that would become the Bill of Rights. Courtesy of the Library of Congress.

Anti-Federalists argued that without a bill of rights, the central government might eventually take away individual rights. The Federalists, however, argued that there was no need to spell out individual rights since the new government could only exercise those powers expressed in the Constitution.

According to Article VII of the Constitution, a minimum of nine of the thirteen states had to ratify the document before it could go into effect. In the months that followed the convention, Anti-Federalists continued to raise the issue of a bill of rights with the public. Having just fought to get rid of the powerful British government, many citizens were afraid of giving the new government too much power without some sort of declaration of the people's rights.

Federalists initially argued against the inclusion of a bill of rights. But in order to win approval for the new constitution, they eventually promised that Congress would add a bill of rights to the Constitution during its first session.

The first amendments: Crafting the Bill of Rights

The Federalists kept their word. From the hundreds of proposals made by the states, James Madison, now a representative to the House, drafted seventeen amendment proposals, which he presented to Congress

Introduction

on June 8, 1789. Over the next three months, Congress revised Madison's suggestions into twelve amendment proposals, which were then passed to the states for ratification. While the states were considering the proposed amendments, Vermont became the fourteenth state on March 4, 1791. Under the rules set out in the Constitution, this meant that eleven states (three-fourths of the existing states) were needed to ratify the constitutional amendments.

Though two of the proposed amendments were rejected (one would later become the Twenty-seventh Amendment), on December 15, 1791, Virginia became the eleventh state to approve the ten amendments that became the Bill of Rights. These amendments set out specific limits to the exercise of government power while guaranteeing certain rights to citizens, especially in regard to court and police actions.

- The First Amendment prohibits Congress from passing any law that abridges (decreases) the existing freedom of speech, religion, or the press (the media).

- The Second Amendment guarantees the "people's right to keep and bear arms [weapons]."

- The Third Amendment limits the government's ability to quarter (or house) soldiers in private homes.

- The Fourth Amendment prohibits unreasonable search and seizure.

- The Fifth Amendment includes several protections for people accused of crimes, including protection against "double jeopardy" (being tried twice for the same crime) and the right not to testify against oneself in trial.

- The Sixth Amendment provides the right to a speedy trial by jury in criminal cases.

- The Seventh Amendment provides for jury trials in civil cases.

- The Eighth Amendment prohibits the setting of excessive bail and fines, and forbids cruel and unusual punishments.

- The Ninth Amendment states that the rights listed in the Constitution are not the only rights retained by the people.

- The Tenth Amendment states that any powers not specifically granted to the federal government are retained by the states and the people, unless the Constitution specifically prohibits the use of such powers.

The Changing Constitution: Proposing and Ratifying Constitutional Amendments

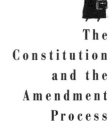
Those first additions and changes to the Constitution were made according to rules spelled out in the Constitution. In fact, Article V of the Constitution sets out two methods for amending the Constitution.

In the first method, Congress may propose an amendment with a two-thirds vote of both the Senate and the House of Representatives. If the proposal passes in both houses, the amendment must then be ratified by three-fourths of the states, either in state-wide conventions or by votes in the states' legislatures (law-making assemblies).

Under the second method, Congress can call for a constitutional convention for the proposal of new amendments. Congress can call for such a convention only if the legislatures from at least two-thirds of the states request that Congress do so.

Any proposals drafted at such a convention must then be ratified by three-fourths of the states. To date, however, the Constitution has only been amended through the first method.

Amending the Constitution is quite difficult. It requires an enormous degree of consensus (agreement) at the state and federal level. The

Abraham Lincoln worked to ensure the emancipation of slaves from their owners. Courtesy of the Library of Congress.

Introduction

framers of the Constitution wanted to make sure that changes to the government were not made lightly. Indeed, in the two hundred-plus years since the Bill of Rights was ratified, only seventeen other amendments have been adopted by the states.

- The Eleventh Amendment (1798) prohibits the Supreme Court from hearing any lawsuits brought against one state by a citizen of another state.

- The Twelfth Amendment (1804) changed the way the president and vice president are elected. The amendment was drafted in response to the election of 1800. At the time, the offices of president and vice president were voted on separately. The party candidate who received the most votes would be president, and the candidate with the next highest number of votes would be vice president. In the election of 1800, one political party's presidential and vice presidential candidates accidentally received the same number of electoral votes for president, causing a great deal of confusion over who would serve as president.

- The Thirteenth (1865), Fourteenth (1868) and Fifteenth (1870) Amendments— which abolished slavery, required states to enforce their laws fairly, and extended the vote to black males—were all passed in the wake of America's bloody Civil War (1860–64) between the Northern and Southern states.

- The Sixteenth Amendment (1913) overrode a technicality in the Constitution, and made it legal for the federal government to implement an income tax.

- The Seventeenth Amendment (1913) provides for the direct election of senators by voters in each state. The Constitution originally gave state legislatures the power to appoint a state's senators.

- The Eighteenth (1919) and Twenty-first Amendments (1933) reflected America's changing attitudes toward alcoholic beverages. The Eighteenth Amendment outlawed the sale and transportation of liquor in the United States, reflecting the nation's growing temperance (anti-alcohol) movement. By 1933, though, American attitudes toward the sale of alcohol had shifted again, and the Twenty-first Amendment repealed (reversed) the ban on liquor.

- The Nineteenth Amendment (1920) extended the vote to women, after nearly a century of vigorous campaigning for female suffrage (the right to vote).

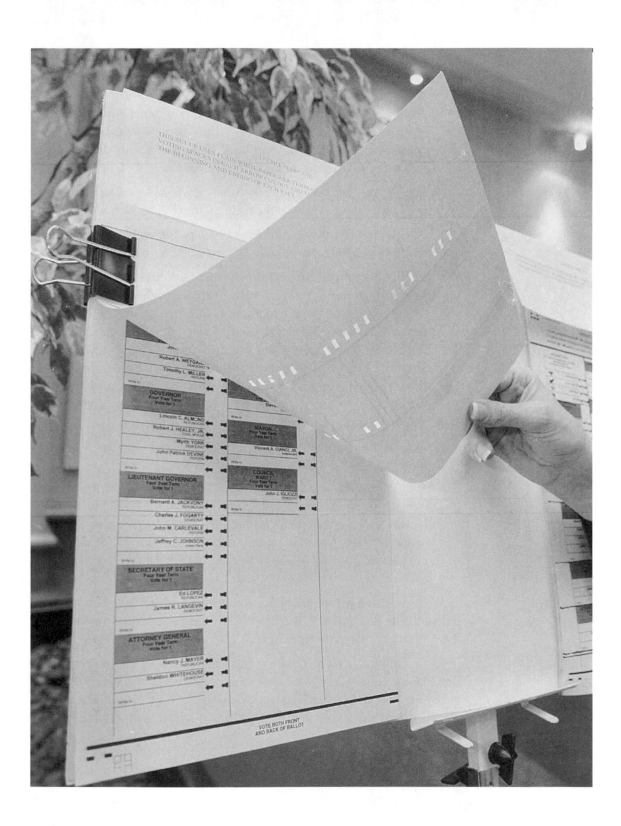

- The Twentieth Amendment (1933) shortened the period between the time a person was elected to federal office and the time he or she took office.

- The Twenty-second Amendment (1951) prohibited any person from being elected to more than two terms as president, and was proposed after the death of Franklin D. Roosevelt, who was elected to four successive terms, beginning with the election of 1932.

- The Twenty-third Amendment (1961) gave residents of Washington D.C. (the nation's capital) the right to vote in presidential elections.

- The Twenty-fourth Amendment (1964) put an end to the practice of charging people a fee, or poll tax, to cast their vote in an election.

- The Twenty-fifth Amendment (1967) granted the president the power to nominate a new vice president whenever that office becomes vacant. The amendment also provides for the vice president to take over a president's duties when the president cannot perform those duties due to poor health or injury. This amendment was passed in the wake of the assassination of President John F. Kennedy in 1961. Vice President Lyndon B. Johnson assumed the presidency, leaving the vice president's office vacant for the remainder of the term.

- The Twenty-sixth Amendment (1971) lowered the legal voting age from twenty-one to eighteen in all elections.

- The Twenty-seventh Amendment (1992) was one of the original twelve amendments proposed for the Bill of Rights in 1789. However, the amendment, which prohibits any pay raise Congress votes for itself from taking effect until the following election, was not ratified until the 1990s, when the issue became a popular political issue.

Additionally, Congress has passed a number of proposals for amendments that failed to be ratified by the necessary three-fourths of the states (see chapter twenty-eight).

Certainly, the Constitution's enduring power is due in part to the fact that the framers provided a method of amending the document when necessary. What is remarkable in discussing the Constitutional amendments, however, is how very rarely the American people have found it necessary to do so.

Constitutional Amendments

Ninth Amendment

The enumeration in the Constitution, of certain rights, shall not be construed to deny or disparage others retained by the people.

The Bill of Rights is primarily a list of restrictions on the government, preventing it from acting against the people's rights. When the idea of adding a bill of rights to the Constitution was first brought up, many people argued against it. Some people felt such a list wasn't needed because the Constitution specifically lists what actions the government can take. In other words, because the government can only do the things the Constitution gives it the power to do, a list of things it can't do serves no real purpose.

At the time the Constitution was adopted, the public was largely in favor of a bill of rights that would specifically protect certain rights. But creating a list of rights raised another concern. Opponents of a bill of rights worried that listing some of the rights might lead the government to take away or trample on any rights that weren't listed.

The Ninth Amendment was written to address that worry. It states that the listing of certain rights in the Constitution "shall not be construed (understood) to deny or disparage (discredit) others retained by the people." In other words, the amendment states that the Bill of Rights should in no way be considered a complete list of people's rights.

Edmund Randolph (1753–1813), a politician from Virginia, argued that the amendment was meaningless. He warned that the rights in the first eight amendments "were not all that a free people would require" but felt that the Ninth Amendment was too weak to guarantee other rights. To some extent, Randolph's predictions came true. Because the Ninth Amendment doesn't list specific rights, it has played a role in only a handful of Supreme Court cases since its adoption.

RATIFICATION FACTS

PROPOSED: Submitted by Congress to the states on September 25, 1789.

RATIFICATION: Ratified by the required three-fourths of states (11 of 14) on December 15, 1791. Declared to be part of the Constitution on December 15, 1791.

RATIFYING STATES: Ratifying states: New Jersey, November 20, 1789; Maryland, December 19, 1789; North Carolina, December 22, 1789; South Carolina, January 19, 1790; New Hampshire, January 25, 1790; Delaware, January 28, 1790; New York, February 24, 1790; Pennsylvania, March 10, 1790; Rhode Island, June 7, 1790; Vermont, November 3, 1791; Virginia, December 15, 1791 (amendment adopted).

But the Ninth Amendment served two valuable roles. First, it eased fears that the Bill of Rights might be used to limit people's rights rather than protect them. Second, it serves as a formal reminder that the government's powers are limited to those granted to it by the Constitution — and that the government has no power beyond those listed in the Constitution to limit the individual's rights.

Origins of the Ninth Amendment

In 1775, war broke out between Great Britain and its thirteen American colonies. At the conclusion of the American Revolutionary War in 1783, the colonies had won their independence, and the newly independent states united under the terms of a document known as the Articles of Confederation.

Under the Articles of Confederation, the states kept most governmental powers while the federal (central) government was given very little power to act on its own. Within a few years, it became apparent that the new nation would require a more powerful central government, especially when dealing with foreign countries. In 1787, representatives from twelve of the states were sent to a Constitutional Convention in Philadelphia, Pennsylvania, where they worked to create a constitution for a new federal government.

In 1788, the states adopted the U.S. Constitution (see chapter one), which established a strong national government with power divided among a powerful president, Congress (the legislative or lawmaking body of government), and the Supreme Court.

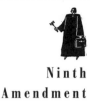

Arguments against a bill of rights

Although many state constitutions featured a bill of rights (a list of the people's rights that were protected from government interference) nothing in the new Constitution spelled out the people's rights. Backers of the new Constitution (known as Federalists) argued that such a bill of rights was unnecessary because the new government would only have the powers given to it by the Constitution. For instance, because the Constitution did not give Congress the power to regulate the press or the church, there was no need to for an amendment that protected freedom of the press or freedom of religion.

The Federalists were not against limiting the government's powers. In fact, many of them were worried that a bill of rights would actually give the government more power. Alexander Hamilton (1755–1804) was a prominent Federalist and opposed a bill of rights. In an essay in favor of the new Constitution, he argued that a list of rights was "not only unnecessary in the proposed Constitution but would even be dangerous."

Hamilton (who later became the nation's first secretary of the Treasury under George Washington), and others argued that listing some rights might give the government an excuse to take away rights that weren't listed. As James Wilson (1742–1798) a prominent Federalist politician from Pennsylvania, put it: "Enumerate all the rights of men! I am sure, sir, that no gentleman would have attempted such a thing. To every suggestion concerning a bill of rights, the citizens of the United States may always say, "We reserve the right to do what we please."

Federalist Theodore Sedgwick (1746–1813) of Massachusetts, who served in the House of Representatives, jokingly asked whether the Anti-Federalists thought it was necessary for Congress to have "declared that a man should have a right to wear his hat if he pleased; that he might get up when he pleased, and to go to bed when he thought proper."

The argument in favor of a bill of rights

Opponents of the new Constitution (Anti-Federalists) nonetheless argued that without a bill of rights, the new government would eventually trample the people's rights. George Mason (1725–1792), a leading

A CASE OF MISTAKEN IDENTITY

Other than the Third Amendment (see chapter three) the Ninth Amendment has had less impact on Supreme Court decisions than any of the other Bill of Rights amendment. To add insult to injury, the first time the Supreme Court referred to the amendment, it was a mistake.

In *Lessee of Livingston v. Moore* (1833), the court discussed the Ninth "Article" of the constitutional amendments, but the court was actually referring to the Seventh Amendment. It's possible the justices on the court were inadvertently referring to the ninth *proposed* amendment.

James Madison (1751–1836) had written seventeen proposals for the Bill of Rights. Congress, however, only passed twelve of those proposals, and the states in turn ratified just ten. The case involved the right to a jury trial, which is protected by the Seventh Amendment, but which was the *ninth* amendment proposed to the states. Alas, the real Ninth Amendment would not play a significant role in a case for more than 130 more years.

Anti-Federalist from Virginia, had attended the Constitutional Convention but refused to sign the document because it had no bill of rights. Mason argued that the Articles of Confederation had declared that "Each state retains its sovereignty, freedom and independence, and every power, jurisdiction and right, which is not expressly delegated to the United States, in Congress assembled."

"Why not have a similar clause in this Constitution," Mason wondered. The lack of such a clause seemed to suggest that the new government was not limited in any way.

Patrick Henry (1736–1799), a well-known revolutionary leader from Virginia, agreed with Mason. "If you intend to reserve your unalienable rights," Henry declared, "you must have the most express stipulation (of those rights)."

The Anti-Federalists lost the fight against the new Constitution, but managed to raise the public's concern over the absence of a Bill of Rights. The states voted to adopt the new Constitution in 1788. But Congress (the lawmaking body of the new federal government) immediately began drafting a bill of rights once the Constitution was in place.

Filling the "dangerous" gap

James Madison (1751–1836), a Virginia lawyer who later became the fourth president of the United States, was one of Virginia's representatives in the House of Representatives in Congress. Madison had been a strong supporter of the new Constitution, but by 1789 he had come to support the addition of a bill of rights.

Madison wrote the original drafts of all ten of the Bill of Rights amendments. But Madison agreed with other Federalists about the danger that a list of rights might imply that the people were only entitled to the rights listed.

"This is one of the most plausible arguments I have ever heard against the admission of a bill of rights into the system," he said, "but I conceive, that it may be guarded against."

Madison proposed an amendment stating that "[t]he exceptions here or elsewhere in the Constitution, made in favor of particular rights, shall not be so construed (understood) as to diminish the just importance of other rights retained by the people, or as to enlarge the powers delegated (to the government) by the Constitution; but either as actual limitations of such powers, or as inserted merely for greater caution."

Madison's wording was edited in Congress to its final simpler form: The enumeration in the Constitution, of certain rights, shall not be construed to deny or disparage others retained by the people.

While not all Federalists or Anti-Federalists were satisfied with the amendment, its inclusion in the Bill of Rights served as a reminder that the people's rights were not limited to those listed in the other amendments. And the amendment also helped ease fears that a Bill of Rights would give the government more power, not less.

The Ninth Amendment became part of the Constitution on December 15, 1791, when Virginia became the twelfth state (of the existing fourteen) to ratify the first ten so-called Bill of Rights amendments to the U.S. Constitution.

Supreme Court Stays Mum on Unenumerated Rights

The Constitution established the Supreme Court of the United States as the nation's highest court. The Court originally consisted of six justices

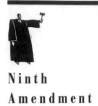

Ninth Amendment

(judges), but since 1869, has included nine justices. A justice may write an opinion supporting either side of a given case, but the court's final ruling is left to a simple vote of all the justices. The justices typically hear appeals of cases first heard by lower courts. An appeal is a legal request to reconsider a court's ruling.

The Supreme Court holds the final power to interpret the country's laws, including the Constitution and its amendments. And yet the Court has rarely tried to interpret the Ninth Amendment. In the first 160 years after the passage of the Bill of Rights, the Supreme Court heard very few cases involving the Ninth Amendment. And even in those cases, the court shed little light on what rights, if any, the Ninth Amendment protected.

Granted powers trump Ninth Amendment rights

In *Ashwander v. Tennessee Valley Authority* (1936), the Supreme Court described rights that were *not* protected by the amendment.

"[T]he Ninth Amendment does not withdraw the rights that are expressly granted to the federal government," the Court ruled. In other words, while the people may have rights that are not spelled out in the Constitution, no such rights can interfere with the government's right to do what the Constitution specifically says it may do.

So in *Tennessee Electric Power Co. v. Tennessee Valley Authority* (1939) the Court ruled that the Ninth Amendment did not prevent the federal government from controlling the retail price of its electrical energy. In that case, public utilities (power companies) claimed that the government was interfering with their right to acquire property and use it in lawful business.

But the Court ruled that Congress had the constitutional right to regulate the prices because that power existed within "the generally existing conception of governmental powers." Because those powers were granted to Congress by the Constitution, the Ninth Amendment could not be used to override them.

In *Woods v. Miller* (1948) the Supreme Court ruled again that there were no "unenumerated rights" in cases where the Constitution gave Congress the power to act. In the case, landlords argued that laws passed during World War II (which the United States participated in from 1941–1945) violated their Ninth Amendment rights — rights that existed even thought they weren't set out in the Constitution.

But the Court ruled that because the Constitution granted Congress far-reaching powers during times of war, the laws did not take away any Ninth Amendment rights the landlords might have claimed.

Fourteen vs. Nine: Due Process and the People's Rights

One of the reasons the Ninth Amendment has played such a small role in constitutional cases is that the Supreme Court has often used the Fourteenth Amendment (ratified in 1868) to establish broader rights for the people (see chapter fourteen.)

The Fourteenth Amendment's due process and equal protection clauses require federal and state governments to treat all citizens equally and fairly. The Supreme Court has used this clause to establish civil rights (see chapter fourteen) and to strike down laws that violate certain individual rights, including those that are not specifically spelled out in the Constitution.

In *Skinner v. Oklahoma* (1942), for instance, the court used the Fourteenth Amendment's equal protection clause to uphold a person's right to procreate (have children). Although the right to procreate is not listed anywhere in the Bill of Rights or the rest of the Constitution, the court found that the right was protected by the Fourteenth Amendment. Interestingly, the ruling did not even mention the Ninth Amendment.

The Right to Privacy

The Ninth Amendment was first used by the Supreme Court to define an "unenumerated right" in the case of *Griswold v. Connecticut* (1965). The right to privacy is not referred to anywhere in the Bill of Rights. However, in deciding *Griswold* the court found that the right was indeed protected by the Constitution.

The case involved a Connecticut law that made it illegal for people to use contraceptives (birth control devices). Estelle T. Griswold, executive director of the Planned Parenthood League of Connecticut, and C. Lee Buxton, a doctor at the Planned Parenthood Center in New Haven, had given out contraceptives to clients for ten days before being arrested on November 10, 1961.

Griswold and Buxton were convicted in a Connecticut court and fined one hundred dollars each. However, the U.S. Supreme Court agreed to hear the case on appeal. (An appeal is a legal request to reconsider a lower court's decision.)

The Supreme Court found that the Connecticut law was unconstitutional. The majority of the Court's nine justices ruled (for the first time) that the Constitution guaranteed a right to privacy. This right, according to the court, was suggested in the margins of the Bill of Rights in the First, Third, Fourth, Fifth, and Ninth Amendments (see chapters one, three, four and five.)

Although the Court relied on other amendments as well, this was the first case where the Ninth Amendment played a significant role in the court's deliberations. Justice Arthur Goldberg (1908–1990) (see sidebar) wrote specifically about the importance of the Ninth Amendment in the case. He noted that "since 1791 [the Ninth Amendment] has been a basic part of the Constitution which we are sworn to uphold. To hold that a right so basic and fundamental and so deep-rooted in our society as the right to privacy in marriage may be infringed because that right is not guaranteed in so many words by the first eight amendments to the Constitution is to ignore the Ninth Amendment and give it no effect whatsoever."

Planned Parenthood continues to aid people in their search for information on reproduction and contraception.

Reproduced by permission of AP/Wide World Photos.

Following the *Griswold* case, the Supreme Court began to extend the right to privacy, especially in sexual and marital issues. In *Loving v. Virginia* (1967), the Court struck down a Virginia law that banned interracial marriages. The court later strengthened the *Griswold* ruling in *Eisenstadt v. Baird* (1972). In that case, the Court threw out a Massachusetts statute that permitted married people to use condoms (a birth control device) but did not allow single people to use them.

Roe v. Wade: Privacy and Abortion

In the 1850s, the American Medical Association (AMA) urged state legislatures (lawmaking bodies) to outlaw abortion, primarily because the procedures used at the time were considered quite dangerous. (Abortion is a medical procedure in which a fetus is terminated or removed from a woman's body before it can live on its own.) By 1900, most states had made abortion illegal. Women who wished to end their pregnancies often found doctors to perform illegal abortions or chose to have dangerous abortions performed by unskilled people.

By the 1950s and 1960s, new medical procedures had made abortions much safer. Because abortions were still illegal, however, many women were still risking highly dangerous abortions. Many professional groups, including the AMA, announced that they now supported the legalization of abortion, and a few states got rid of their antiabortion laws.

On March 3, 1970, Norma McCorvey filed suit in a federal district court challenging a Texas law that made it illegal for her to have an abortion. McCorvey was six months pregnant at the time. She used the fictitious name "Jane Roe" in the case to avoid unwanted publicity.

The district court agreed that the law violated McCorvey's right to privacy but did not strike down the law to let McCorvey have an abortion. McCorvey gave birth in June 1970 and put her child up for adoption. But she proceeded to take her case to the Supreme Court, arguing that the abortion law violated the right to privacy as recognized by the Court in *Griswold v. Connecticut* (1965).

The Supreme Court ruled on McCorvey's case, known as *Roe v. Wade* on January 22, 1973. The Court found that the right to privacy included a limited right to an abortion. By a vote of seven to two, the Court held that the due process clause of the Fourteenth Amendment, "which protects against state action the right to privacy," included a woman's "qualified right to terminate her pregnancy."

JUSTICE ARTHUR GOLDBERG: BLACK-ROBED CHAMPION OF THE NINTH AMENDMENT

The Ninth Amendment was largely ignored by the Supreme Court for a century and a half. But in the 1965 case of *Griswold v. Connecticut* (see main essay) Justice Arthur Goldberg (1908–1990) tried to give the Ninth Amendment substance.

Estelle Griswold and C. Lee Buxton were convicted under a Connecticut law prohibiting the prescription of contraceptive devices. The Supreme Court overturned their convictions ruling that amendments to the Constitution, especially the First, Third, Fourth, Fifth, and Ninth, acted *together* to create a right to privacy that protected such personal decisions as the use of contraception in a marriage.

Justice Goldberg, who served on the Supreme Court from 1962 to 1965, agreed with the decision but argued that the Court didn't need to look beyond the Ninth Amendment to justify its ruling. The Ninth Amendment asserts that people have rights that are not necessarily spelled out in the Constitution. To determine what these rights are, Goldberg said that judges "must look to the traditions and collective conscience of our people to determine whether a principle is so rooted there as to be ranked as fundamental."

The right to privacy in marriage, Goldberg insisted, was just such a principle and therefore fell under the protection of the Ninth Amendment as a fundamental but unenumerated (unwritten) right.

Although the majority of the Supreme Court justices decided that the right to privacy comes from several amendments and was not protected by the Ninth Amendment alone, Justice Goldberg's arguments helped raise the public's awareness of the Ninth Amendment higher than any other justice had since the amendment's adoption in 1791.

The Court again acknowledged that the Constitution contained no explicit right to privacy. However, the plurality believed that "the roots" of such a right did exist in the "First Amendment, in the Fourth and Fifth Amendments, in the [margins] of the Bill of Rights, in the Ninth Amendment, or in the concept of liberty guaranteed by the first section of the Fourteenth Amendment." (see related chapters.)

The court relied primarily on the due process clause of the Fourteenth Amendment to grant the right to privacy in this case, but it also mentioned the Ninth Amendment. "The right to privacy," Justice Harry Blackmun (1908–1999) wrote, "whether it be founded in the Fourteenth Amendment's concept of personal liberty or in the Ninth Amendment's reservation of rights to the people, is broad enough to encompass a woman's decision whether or not to terminate her pregnancy."

The "right to loaf"

Justice William O. Douglas (1898–1980) also referred to the Ninth Amendment in relation to *Roe v. Wade.*

"The Ninth Amendment obviously does not create federally enforceable rights," Justice Douglas admitted. "But a catalogue of these rights includes customary, traditional, and time-honored rights that come within the sweep of 'the Blessings of Liberty' mentioned in the preamble to the Constitution."

Douglas then listed what he considered to be the fundamental rights that existed under the Ninth Amendment:

"First is the autonomous (independent) control over the development and expression of one's intellect, interests, tastes, and personality."

"Second is the freedom of choice in the basic decisions of one's life respecting marriage, divorce, procreation, contraception, and the education and upbringing of children."

"Third is the freedom to care for one's health and person, freedom from bodily restraint or compulsion, freedom to walk, stroll, or loaf."

These fundamental rights, Justice Douglas conceded, were "subject to regulation on a showing of 'compelling state interest.'" The Court, however, never adopted Douglas's listing of the Ninth Amendment's unenumerated rights.

Court finds unenumerated rights without Ninth Amendment

As mentioned above, the Supreme Court has established a number of unenumerated rights, but has routinely relied on its interpretation of the Fourteenth Amendment to do so and generally ignored the Ninth.

The Court has refused to say that the Ninth Amendment guarantees the right of people to engage in homosexual activities (sexual relations

**Ninth
Amendment**

*Basic decisions such
as who we marry
are considered
fundamental rights.*
Reproduced by permission of
AP/Wide World Photos.

between people of the same sex). However, in *Romer v. Evans* (1996),
the Supreme Court ruled that amendments to Colorado's constitution that
forbade the state and local governments from passing laws to protect the
civil rights of gays, lesbians, and bisexuals violated the equal protection
clause of the Fourteenth Amendment.

The U.S. Supreme Court has also found that the right to vote and
the right to participate in politics are protected by the Fourteenth Amendment, despite the fact that they are not specifically mentioned in that
amendment.

The Supreme Court has also found that other rights do not exist within the Constitution. The Court ruled, for instance that the right to a public education is not a fundamental constitutional right in *San Antonio Independent School District v. Rodriguez* [1993]). Nor is the right to resist military draft, *United States v. Uhl* (9th Cir. 1970); the right to a radiation-free environment, *Concerned Citizens of Nebraska v. U.S. Nuclear Regulatory Commission* (8th Cir. 1992); or the right to experiment with mind-altering drugs such as marijuana, *United States v. Fry* (4th Cir. 1986).

However, in all these case, the Court relied on other parts of the Constitution to reach its conclusions and did not rely on the Ninth Amendment for guidance.

The Ninth Amendment's Legacy

After Justice Goldberg focused attention on it in *Griswold v. Connecticut*, the amendment gradually faded from view. Indeed, because the Ninth Amendment is so vague, it has never been used by itself in a Supreme Court case decision.

The Supreme Court has not ruled on whether or not the Ninth Amendment guarantees the right of people to engage in homosexual activities. Reproduced by permission of Cathy Cade.

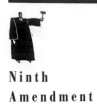

**Ninth
Amendment**

But it should be remembered that the amendment was intended to be vague. In fact, it is probably best understood as a statement of fact, rather than as a useful legal tool. The role of the Ninth Amendment was not to spell out certain rights, but to formally state that the people had more rights than were contained in the other Bill of Rights amendments.

And though the Supreme Court has rarely used the Ninth Amendment to find these unenumerated rights in the Constitution, it has repeatedly established the existence of such rights under the Fourteenth Amendment.

Perhaps the Ninth Amendment's most important role was its first. By assuring the public that the Bill of Rights was not supposed to be a complete list of the people's rights, it helped win over many of the Bill of Rights opponents and ease its eventual ratification by the states.

For More Information

Books

Black, Charles L. *A New Birth of Freedom: Human Rights, Named and Unnamed.* New York: Grosset/Putnam, 1997, 175.

Bryner, Gary C., and A. D. Sorensen, eds. *The Bill of Rights: A Bicentennial Assessment.* Provo, UT: Brigham Young University, 1994, 280.

Curie, David P. *The Constitution of the United States: A Primer for the People.* Chicago: University of Chicago, 1988, 134.

Landau, Elaine. *Your Legal Rights: From Custody Battles to School Searches—the Headline Making Cases that Affect Your Life.* New York: Walter & Company, 84.

McWhirter, Darien A., and Jon D. Bible. *Privacy as a Constitutional Right: Sex, Drugs, and the Right to Life.* New York: Quorom Books, 1992, 206.

Stein, R. Conrad. *The Story of the Powers of the Supreme Court.* Chicago: Childrens Press, 1989, 32.

Web sites

FindLaw Internet Legal Resources. *U.S. Supreme Court Opinions.* [Online] http://www.findlaw.com/casecode/supreme.html (accessed on January 24, 2000.)

Ride, Sally. "American Perspectives: The Ninth Amendment." *Mighty Words.* [Online] http://www1.mightywords.com/freedom (accessed on May 16, 2000.)

Sources

Caplan, Russell L. "The History and Meaning of the Ninth Amendment." *Virginia Law Review* 69 (March 1983): 223–68.

Curie, David P. *The Constitution of the United States: A Primer for the People.* Chicago: University of Chicago, 1988, 134.

Encyclopedia of World Biography. 17 vols. Detroit: Gale Research, 1998.

Kickok, Jr., Eugene W., ed. *The Bill of Rights: Original Meaning and Current Understanding.* Charlottesville, VA: University Press of Virginia, 1991, 473.

Kinsella, N. Stephan. "Taking the Ninth Amendment Seriously: A Review of Calvin R. Massey's Silent Rights: The Ninth Amendment and the Constitution's Unenumerated Rights." *Hastings Constitutional Law Quarterly* 24 (spring 1997): 757–63.

Klinkner, Philip A. *The American Heritage History of the Bill of Rights: The Ninth Amendment.* Englewood Cliffs, NJ: Silver Burdett Press, 1991.

Levinson, Sanford. "Constitutional Rhetoric and the Ninth Amendment." *Chicago-Kent Law Review* 64 (1988): 131, 134.

Marks, Jason S. "Beyond Penumbras and Emanations: Fundamental Rights, the Spirit of the Revolution, and the Ninth Amendment," *Seton Hall Constitutional Law Journal* 5 (spring 1995): 435–787.

Matheson, Cameron S. "The Once and Future Ninth Amendment." *Boston College Law Review* 38 (December 1996): 179–204.

Patterson, Bennett B. *The Forgotten Ninth Amendment.* Indianapolis, IN: Bobbs-Merrill Company, 1955.

"Report to the Attorney General." U.S. Department of Justice Office of Legal Policy September 25, 1987.

Thapa, Tejshree. "Expounding the Constitution: Legal Fictions and the Ninth Amendment." *Cornell Law Review* 78 (November 1992): 139–40.

West's Encyclopedia of American Law. 12 vols. St. Paul, Minn.: West Group, 1998.

Tenth Amendment

The powers not delegated to the United States by the Constitution, nor prohibited by it to the States, are reserved to the States respectively, or to the people.

The United States government collects taxes, holds elections, regulates businesses, and sets environmental standards for the nation. It builds roads, creates and enforces laws, settles law suits, and holds criminal trials. But state governments also do all of these things. Under the U.S. system of "dual sovereignty" (two governments), the federal and state governments share the power to govern. Inevitably, conflicts have arisen between the two governments. The question of where to draw the line between state and national authority was the center of debate during the drafting of the Constitution. Later, it nearly broke up the United States with the breakout of the Civil War (1861–1865).

The Tenth Amendment was written to help define the relationship between both governments. The amendment does not specifically list the powers that belong to the states or to the federal government. Therefore, the Tenth Amendment has always been wide open to a variety of interpretations. And different interpretations have led to dramatic shifts in the balance of power between the states and the federal government.

Origins of the Tenth Amendment

In 1775, Britain's thirteen American colonies each had separate identities with diverse histories, religious traditions, and unique economies. Manufacturing, shipping, and small farms were dominate professions in the northern colonies. Most men were farmers, merchants, or paid laborers.

RATIFICATION FACTS

PROPOSED: Submitted by Congress to the states on September 25, 1789, along with the other nine amendments that comprise the Bill of Rights.

RATIFICATION: Ratified by the required three-fourths of states (eleven of fourteen) on December 15, 1791. Declared to be part of the Constitution on December 15, 1791.

RATIFYING STATES: New Jersey, November 20, 1789; Maryland, December 19, 1789; North Carolina, December 22, 1789; South Carolina, January 19, 1790; New Hampshire, January 25, 1790; Delaware, January 28, 1790; New York, February 24, 1790; Pennsylvania, March 10, 1790; Rhode Island, June 7, 1790; Vermont, November 3, 1791; Virginia, December 15, 1791 (amendment adopted).

In the southern colonies, on the other hand, commercial crops were the main economy. Crops such as cotton and tobacco were raised on huge plantations (commercial farms) that depended heavily on the labor of African American slaves.

The colonies were settled largely by immigrants from England, Ireland, and Scotland, and thus had a great deal in common. They shared many common institutions imported from England, like the jury trial and colonial legislatures (law-making bodies) made up of elected representatives. Another common bond they shared was that Parliament (the British legislature) had the power to overrule the colonial legislatures. This meant Parliament could impose laws and regulations on the colonies without their consent.

A nation comes together

Throughout the 1700s, issues such as taxation, tariffs, and the presence of the British Army in the colonies (see chapter three) led to growing tensions between the colonies and the British government. The colonies eventually drew together. They boycotted British goods, staged large protests against British polices, and eventually went to war with Britain in 1775. When the American Revolutionary War ended in 1783, the American colonies had won their independence.

Tenth Amendment

The newly independent American states weren't eager to put themselves under another powerful central government. The states created a formal union with one another under the Articles of Confederation (1781). They intentionally created a weak central government, and kept most government power at the state level.

Buffing up the national government: the Constitutional Convention of 1787

Under the Articles of Confederation, the new nation found it was difficult to deal with other countries. The weak central government could not speak with a strong national voice on matters of trade and foreign relations. In May of 1787, the states sent representatives to the Constitutional Convention in Philadelphia, Pennsylvania to come up with a plan for strengthening the national government.

The Convention was dominated by debates between Federalists, who favored a strong central government, and Anti-Federalists, who favored strong state governments (see Introduction). The Constitution that emerged from these debates created a system of "dual sovereignty" (two powers): the federal and state governments would both exercise government powers. So where did one government's powers end and the other's begin? The Constitution only hints at the answer.

Three branches: the federal powers.

The Constitution divides the federal government into three branches: the executive branch, the judicial branch, and the legislative branch. The executive branch is headed by the president, and carries out federal policies. The judicial branch is headed by the Supreme Court (see below), and settles matters of national law. The legislative branch is embodied in the U.S. Congress, and creates the nations laws. Section 8 of Article I of the Constitution (see Introduction) enumerates (lists) Congress's powers, including the powers to:

- raise taxes for the "defense and general welfare of the United States" (General Welfare Clause)

- regulate commerce "with other nations and between the states" (Commerce Clause)

- regulate naturalization (the process by which foreigners can become citizens)

- create and regulate a national currency (money)

- establish a postal system

- create courts beneath the Supreme Court

- declare war and maintain an army and navy

- make all laws "necessary and proper" for carrying out the powers granted to the United States government by the Constitution.

This description of powers, however, with vague terms like "general welfare" and "necessary and proper" left the exact powers of the Congress open to wide interpretation.

To list or not to list

The new Constitution was ratified (approved) by the states in 1788, and George Washington (1732–1799) took office as the first president of the United States in 1789. But Anti-Federalists and the public at large were still wary of the new federal government's power. One of the biggest concerns was that the Constitution contained no bill of rights. A bill of rights is a list of individual rights that cannot be violated by the government.

Federalists argued that since the government could only do those things the Constitution said it could do, it wasn't necessary to also list the things it *couldn't* do. But public uproar persuaded the Federalists to draft a bill of rights during Congress's first session.

James Madison (1751–1836) was the main author of the Constitution, and a representative to Congress from Virginia. Madison drafted proposals for all of the Bill of Rights amendments (see Introduction), including the Tenth Amendment. The Tenth Amendment was designed to ease the public's fear by assuring them that once the federal government was firmly in place, it would not try to expand its powers beyond those given to it by the Constitution.

The amendment states that any powers not granted to the federal government in the Constitution are reserved (and can only be claimed) by the states and the people. However, the Tenth Amendment does not state which powers those are. (See sidebar.)

Defining Necessary and Proper

The Tenth Amendment was passed by Congress on September 25, 1789, and officially ratified by the states on December 15, 1791. But

Tenth
Amendment

THE IMPORTANCE OF IMPLIED POWER

When Madison made his proposal for the Tenth Amendment, Anti-Federalists wanted to limit the federal government's powers as much as possible. They argued the amendment should state that: those powers not *expressly* delegated to the United States by the Constitution ... are reserved to the States. The use of the term "expressly delegated" would have limited the federal government to those powers and actions *specifically* enumerated in the Constitution, and would have given the states all other governmental power.

Madison and other Federalists objected to the word "expressly." They believed that the government had two kinds of powers: express and implied. Express powers were those powers specifically enumerated in the Constitution. Implied powers, on the other hand, were those powers that the Constitution only suggested, or hinted at.

Imagine a man hires you to watch his dog while he goes out of town. Before he leaves, he gives you three instructions: feed the dog twice a day, walk it in the local park every night, and, generally, take care of the dog. These are your "express" duties. However, to take care

even before the amendment was ratified, the extent of the federal government's powers came into question.

The Federalist's interpretation

Federalists tended to favor a broad interpretation of federal powers. Secretary of Treasury Alexander Hamilton (1755–1804) was a devoted Federalist. Early in 1791, Hamilton proposed the creation of a national bank that would issue money, hold deposits of tax dollars, and lend money. The Constitution does not specifically give Congress the power create such a bank. But Hamilton argued that Congress's power to create a bank was implied (see sidebar) in its power to collect taxes and regulate money and commerce.

The Federalist-controlled Congress supported Hamilton's argument, as did President Washington. The first Bank of the United States was created. It put the government's implied powers to use before the Tenth Amendment had even been ratified.

of the dog, you realize you have to exercise a number of implied duties—duties that are only hinted at in the owners instructions. For instance, feeding the dog also means making sure it has enough water. Perhaps the local park requires dogs to be kept on leashes. You have the implied duty to put the dog on a leash. If the dog gets sick, you might even have to take the dog to visit a veterinarian. Although the owner did not spell out any of these duties, they were all implied in his original instructions.

According to Madison, the Framers (or writers) of the Constitution could not possibly list every single action the federal government might need to take while doing its duties. Instead, it was necessary for the government to exercise (put to use) certain implied powers in order to perform its express powers. Congress was dominated by Federalists (people who favored a strong central government) at the time. They passed the amendment without the word "expressly" in it.

However, the Tenth Amendment could not express the government's implied powers any more than the Constitution could. The question of which powers were implied by the Constitution, in particular the Commerce Clause (which gave Congress the power to regulate commerce), continued to fuel debates over the reach of federal and state powers.

The Democratic-Republican's interpretation

Others in the country favored a more limited interpretation of federal power. Secretary of State Thomas Jefferson (1743–1826) opposed the national bank. He did not believe it was necessary to the federal government. He argued that the Constitution's Necessary and Proper Clause limited Congress to those laws that were *necessary,* not simply "convenient."

Jefferson, a Virginian, was elected president in 1800. He was the first in a string of six consecutive presidents from the Democratic-Republican Party (later known as the Democratic Party). Many Democratic-Republicans had been Anti-Federalist, and tended to favor state rights.

In 1817, President James Madison was now a Democratic-Republican. He vetoed a federal bill to construct roads and canals that would promote commercial activity between the states. Madison argued that the power to make the improvements did not appear "among the enumerated powers" in the Constitution. He also did not find that "any just interpretation" of the Necessary and Proper Clause gave the federal government such powers.

**Tenth
Amendment**

The Supreme Court's interpretation

Of course the ultimate power to interpret the Constitution and its amendments belongs to the Supreme Court of the United States, the nation's highest court. The Court consisted of six justices (judges) until 1869 when it was expanded to include nine justices. Justices may write opinions supporting either side of a case, but the Court's final ruling comes down to a vote of the justices.

In *McCulloch v. Maryland* (1819), the Court ruled in favor of a broad interpretation of the Necessary and Proper Clause, and limited the states use of the Tenth Amendment to claim power. Congress had created the Second Bank of the United States in 1816. (In this case, President Madison approved the expansion of federal powers.) State governments immediately complained that the national bank was competing with their banks. When Maryland attempted to tax the Second Bank, the Bank refused to pay. Maryland then sued James W. McCulloch, a cashier at the Second Bank.

Maryland argued that only the states have the power to create a government-owned bank. Maryland said the Tenth Amendment gives all powers not granted to the federal government to the states, and the Constitution did not give Congress the power to create a bank.

The Court ruled against Maryland. The Court stated that the federal government did indeed have implied powers. The government's creation of a national bank *was* necessary for the collection of taxes, the lending of money, and the regulation of commerce. The Court also ruled that states had "no power, by taxation or otherwise" to interfere with "the operations of the constitutional laws enacted by Congress... ." Therefore, Maryland could not tax the Second Bank.

This ruling tipped the balance of power in the federal government's favor. But over the next several decades, states would take drastic actions in an attempt to tip the scales back.

The States Push Back

The vast difference between the economies of the North and South was at the center of another battle emerging between state and federal powers. In 1816, Congress passed a national tariff (a tax on imported goods.) The tariff was intended to help U.S. businesses by making foreign goods like wool and cotton more expensive than similar goods produced in the United States. The tariffs helped the northern states, but never did much for the economies of the southern states. In fact, some southern politicians argued that the tariffs actually hurt the South.

When Congress approved an even higher tariff in 1828, the South Carolina legislature drafted a protest document. The document declared that states had the right of "interposition," that is, the right to ignore a federal law. Madison and Jefferson had made similar arguments as far back as 1798. They had argued that if enough states objected to a federal law, the law could be declared null and void. But their ideas hadn't gained much support at the time.

South Carolina revived the idea of nullification by arguing that any state could nullify a federal law that it believed was unconstitutional. As rebellious as the ideas of interposition and nullification seemed, some southern states were discussing an even more drastic action—breaking away from the United States altogether.

Love us or leave us?

In 1832, President Andrew Jackson vetoed a bill to extend the Second Bank of the United States. Rejecting the *McCulloch v. Maryland* decision, Jackson found the bank neither necessary nor proper. By putting

Tenth Amendment

Andrew Jackson's face appears on the twenty dollar bill.
Reproduced by permission of the Corbis Corporation (Bellevue).

an end to the Second Bank, Jackson seemed to come down firmly on the side of state rights.

Also in 1832, Congress passed another tariff act, and South Carolina threatened to secede (break away) from the union. Despite Jackson's respect for state rights, he quickly sent troops to South Carolina to keep order. "Be not deceived by names," Jackson warned the people of South Carolina, "disunion by armed force is treason." Jackson, who had been born in South Carolina, also issued the "Nullification Proclamation." This declared the idea of nullification an "impractical absurdity."

Soon after the crisis in South Carolina, Con-

Dred Scott sued for his freedom after his owner died. Courtesy of the Library of Congress.

gress lowered some tariffs, and South Carolina backed off of its threat to secede. The threat of secession, however, did not disappear. Southern states continued to object to federal actions that they felt infringed upon state rights. Less than thirty years after South Carolina first threatened to secede, the first Civil War (1861–65) battle would be fought on the state's soil.

Slavery and states rights

As mentioned earlier, the southern agricultural economy depended on the use of slaves. From the beginning of the nineteenth century, debate raged between northern "free states" and the southern "slave states" over whether new states should have the right to allow slavery. The nation continued to grow through the first half of the 1800s. Through a series of political compromises, it maintained a nearly perfect balance between slave states and free states.

However, the issue of slavery remained the source of tension between the states. Abolitionists sought to end of slavery in all states. They opposed slavery on moral and economic grounds. Southern states, meanwhile, resented any threat of interference with their most important source of labor (slaves).

In 1857, the Supreme Court heard the case of *Dred Scott v. Sanford*. Scott, a slave from Missouri, had sued for his freedom after his owner died. During the 1830s, Scott had lived with his owner in Illinois and other free northern territories before returning to Missouri. According to Scott, his free status in the northern territories had made him a free man forever.

However, the Supreme Court ruled that Scott was still a slave (and therefore not a U.S. citizen), and did not have the right to sue for his freedom. It also ruled that at the time the Constitution was written, slaves were considered property. The Constitution did not give the federal government the power to take away an owner's property. Under the Tenth Amendment, the Court said, the power to free slaves was reserved for the states.

The Court also ruled that just living in a free state did not make Scott a free man. "As Scott was a slave when taken into the State of Illinois by his owner, and was there held as such, and brought back in that character," the Court said, "his status, as free or slave, depended on the laws of Missouri, and not of Illinois."

The *Dred Scott* decision meant slaves who escaped to free states could legally be captured and returned to their owners. It also meant that the federal government could not interfere with a state's right to allow or abolish slavery. Abolitionists were furious with the decision. Southern states continued to worry about federal interference in state matters. It was little surprise that the issues of slavery and states' rights were at the center of the next presidential election in 1860.

The States Go to War

The struggle to define the relationship between the states and the national government was at the center of the creation of Articles of Confederation, the creation of the Constitution, the passage of the Tenth Amendment, and the decisions of numerous Supreme Court cases. With the outbreak of the Civil War (1861–1865), the struggle turned bloody. In four years, over six hundred thousand Americans were killed. Thousands more were maimed (crippled) or injured in a war that revolved around the issue of states' rights and federal power.

Lincoln defeats three Democrats at once

In the election of 1860, Abraham Lincoln (1809–1865) was the presidential candidate for the new Republican Party. (This party was unrelated to Jefferson's Democratic-Republican Party that was now known simply as the Democratic Party.) Lincoln's party favored a strong federal government, and campaigned on an antislavery platform. "I believe," Lincoln stated, "this government cannot endure permanently half slave and half free."

On the other hand, the Democrats favored states' rights, but had become so divided over the issue of slavery that the party ran two candidates for president. The Constitutional Union Party was made up of former Democrats, and offered yet another candidate (see chapter twelve). Helped by the division in the Democratic Party, Lincoln was elected president.

Secession: the final Tenth Amendment power?

Given the Democrats' power in Congress, it is unlikely Lincoln could have abolished slavery in the Southern states. However, the South had had little luck fighting government's tariffs (see above) even with Southern Democrats in the presidency. The prospect of facing a federal government under an anti-slavery Republican president seemed intolerable. Before Lincoln even took office in March of 1861, seven Southern states (led by South Carolina) seceded from the United States and formed the Confederate States of America, or the Confederacy. (Eventually eleven states joined the Confederacy.)

The Confederate states did not consider secession an act of rebellion. In fact, they argued that leaving the United States was well within the states' legal powers under the Constitution. Jefferson Davis of Virginia (1808–1889) was elected president of the Confederacy. He and other Confederate leaders argued that the states had voluntarily entered the Union when they ratified the Constitution—therefore, it was logical that any state could voluntarily leave it.

Davis also used the Tenth Amendment as a justification for secession. Since the Constitution did not give the federal government any powers to regulate secession (in fact, the Constitution made no mention of secession whatsoever), the Tenth Amendment must grant the power of secession to the states.

Lincoln did not take any direct action against the Confederate states at first. However, he continued to supply federal troops stationed in forts throughout the Southern states. When Lincoln sent military supplies to Fort Sumter in South Carolina, the Confederacy called it an act of war. On April 12, 1861, the Confederate Army opened fire on the Union troops at Fort Sumter, and the Civil War was underway.

During the war, Lincoln took a number of actions that seemed to go far beyond the federal government's established powers over the states. He used state militias to form an army (without Congress's approval). He gave federal officers the power to jail suspected Confederacy sympathizers for indefinite periods of time. And on September 22, 1862, Lincoln issued an executive order that abolished slavery in the Confederate states effective January 1, 1863.

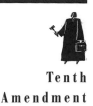
The Civil War amendments

The Confederate Army surrendered to Union forces on April 9, 1865. This brought the Civil War to a close. As one of the conditions for reentering the Union, the Southern states were required to ratify the three

The Battle at Fort Sumter was the beginning of the Civil War. Courtesy of the National Archives and Records Administration.

Tenth Amendment

so-called "Civil War amendments:" the Thirteenth Amendment (see chapter thirteen), the Fourteenth Amendment (see chapter fourteen), and the Fifteenth Amendment (see chapter fifteen).

The Thirteenth Amendment was ratified in 1865. It made slavery illegal throughout the United States "except as punishment for crime."

The Fourteenth Amendment was ratified in 1868. It contained several distinct clauses. The first declared that "[a]ll persons born or naturalized in the United States" are citizens of the United States and of the State they reside in. The Privileges and Immunities Clause prohibits states from making laws that infringe on the "privileges and immunities" that are due to any citizen. The Due Process and Equal Protection Clauses declare that no state may "deprive any person of life, liberty, or property, without due process of law," nor deny a person "equal protection of the laws."

The Fifteenth Amendment was ratified in 1870. It gave all adult males the right to vote, and declared that "[t]he right of citizens of the United States to vote shall not be denied or abridged by the United States or by any State on account of race, color, or previous condition of servitude."

The Civil War amendments represented a decisive change in the relationship between the states and the federal government. The federal government now had powerful Constitutional tools for monitoring the actions of state governments on certain issues. The Fourteenth Amendment's Due Process and Equal Protection Clauses in particular seemed to prohibit the states from passing any laws that discriminated against its citizens.

The Supreme Court and States' Rights After the War

At the end of the nineteenth century, the Supreme Court often took a hands off approach toward state actions—especially in cases that dealt with any sort of discrimination.

The Supreme Court and discrimination cases

The *Slaughter-House Cases* of 1872 dealt with a Louisiana law that gave one New Orleans company the exclusive right to livestock production in the city. Butchers and livestock producers who did not work for this company sued the state. They argued they were being deprived of equal protection of the law that was guaranteed in the Fourteenth Amendment.

The Supreme Court disagreed. The Court said that a state's power to regulate its own affairs "was essential to the perfect working of our complex form of government." The decision in the *Slaughter-House*

Cases seemed to weaken the Fourteenth Amendment, and strengthen the powers reserved to the states by the Tenth Amendment.

The Court also did little to stop states from discriminating on the basis of race or sex, even though the Fourteenth Amendment guaranteed equal protection under the law. In *Bradwell v. Illinois* (1873), the Court ruled that Illinois had the right to prevent women from practicing law. In *Pace v. Alabama* (1883), the Court allowed states to impose more severe penalties for certain sexual crimes if the parties were of different races.

In *Plessy v. Ferguson* (1896), the Court found that state laws could treat blacks and whites separately without violating the Fourteenth Amendment's requirement that states treat all citizens equally. This so-called "separate but equal" decision made it lawful for states to segregate African Americans from European Americans. Segregation was implemented throughout the southern states—in public schools, public transportation, private theaters and restaurants, and even public parks.

The Court and commerce cases

Despite the Supreme Court's protection of state powers, the federal government's powers continued to grow. As the nation became more and more industrialized, commercial activity across state lines increased. In 1887, Congress used its powers under the Commerce Clause to create the Interstate Commerce Commission (ICC). The ICC was a federal agency that actively regulated commercial activity between the states. With federal laws and ICC regulations in place, the federal government's powers within the states grew rapidly.

But even in commerce cases, the Supreme Court acted to limit federal interference in state matters. In *Hammer v. Dagenhart* (1918), for example, the Court struck down a federal law that prohibited products made by children from being transported across state lines. Congress had passed the law using its Commerce Clause powers to regulate interstate commerce. The intent of the law was to discourage child labor. At the time, many young people were put to work in large factories under dangerous and unhealthy conditions.

But the Court ruled that the Commerce Clause did not give Congress the right to restrict the movement of goods unless the goods themselves were harmful. The Court also ruled that Congress's power to regulate commerce only covered the buying, trading, and selling of goods—not the manufacturing of those goods. According to the Court, only states could regulate manufacturing issues—including child labor conditions. Until the end of the 1920s, the Court routinely ruled in favor of state

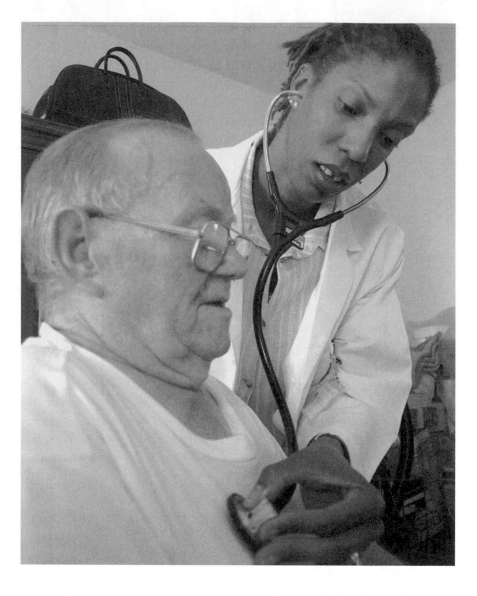

*Part of Roosevelt's
effort to help the
American people
during the Great
Depression was
setting up welfare
programs that
helped the hungry,
the out-of-work,
and those in need
to medical care.*

Reproduced by permission of
AP/Wide World Photos.

powers in commerce cases, and against federal regulations. However,
over the next four decades, there would be a dramatic swing in the
Court's decisions. First in economic matters, and later in the area of civil
rights and racial equality.

FDR and the Rapid Expansion of Federal Power

In the early 1930s, America was hit by the Great Depression which lasted
until the early 1940s. This was an enormous economic slowdown that

affected countries around the world. American businesses suffered great losses. Millions of people were out of work. President Herbert Hoover had been elected in 1928. He resisted creating new federal programs to address the economic downturn. Hoover argued that the economy would naturally correct itself.

But in 1932, Americans elected Franklin Delano Roosevelt (1882–1945) as president, largely because he promised a "new deal" for Americans. Roosevelt pledged to use the federal government's powers to bring the nation out of the depression. In fact, the kinds of federal actions Roosevelt and Congress proposed during his first term as president went far beyond the established limits of federal power at the time.

Under Roosevelt's New Deal programs, the federal government took almost complete control of the national economy. For instance, the National Industrial Recovery Act (NIRA) declared that a "national emergency" existed that "burdens interstate commerce, affects the public welfare, and undermines the standard of living of the American people." NIRA gave Roosevelt the power to approve prices and standards of quality within various industries, and to grant companies licenses to do business. The purpose of the act was to give the federal government the power to improve industrial working conditions, increase employment rates, control wages and prices, and establish fair business practices.

The president and Congress argued that these powers were implied in the federal government's power to collect taxes and regulate interstate commerce. However, the Supreme Court did not interpret the Constitution that way. From 1935 to the spring of 1937, the Court heard ten cases concerning New Deal programs. It struck down programs in eight of those cases.

THE "SICK CHICKEN" CASE. In *Schechter Poultry Corp. v. United States* (1935), the Court used the Tenth Amendment to strike down NIRA. A poultry producer had been convicted of selling sick chickens. This violated regulations set up under NIRA. But the Supreme Court ruled that NIRA could not restrict the selling of these chickens. It then struck down the entire act, stating that the nation's economic hardships "do not create or enlarge constitutional power." In fact, according to the Court, it was just such "emergency" expansions of federal powers that the Tenth Amendment had been written to prevent.

The Court changes its mind

As the Great Depression continued, the Supreme Court began to reverse itself concerning the federal government's power to regulate

Tenth Amendment

business and industry. Roosevelt won a landslide victory in the 1936 presidential election. In 1937, the New Deal's National Labor Relations Act (NLRA) was involved in three separate cases.

In *National Labor Relations Board v. Jones & Laughlin Steel Corp.* (1937), the Court approved a provision of the NLRA that strengthened the power of labor unions to negotiate contracts with employers. (Unions are groups of workers who negotiate wages and working conditions as a group rather than as individuals.)

In *United States v. Darby* (1941), the Court used a very broad interpretation of Congress's Commerce Clause powers. The Court upheld a set of federal laws that established overtime pay and set minimum wages. Since these issues were associated with the manufacturing of goods, the Court essentially overruled its earlier *Hammer v. Dagenhart* decision. The Court ruled that the Tenth Amendment did not deprive the national government of its authority to use any "appropriate" means "for the exercise of a granted power."

The Fourteenth Amendment Eclipses the Tenth Amendment

The Supreme Court's dramatic reinterpretation of the Commerce Clause in the 1930s and 1940s allowed the federal government to increase its regulation of state economic behavior. The Court's equally dramatic reinterpretation of the Fourteenth Amendment in the following decades helped establish the federal government's power to regulate state civil rights laws.

In the 1940s, the federal government officially objected to segregation laws. The Interstate Commerce Commission (ICC) banned discrimination on trains. The Supreme Court supported the decision in *Mitchell v. United States* (1941), and later in *Henderson v. United States* (1950). However, the federal government was forced to use its Commerce Clause powers to attack these laws. This meant that state segregation laws that didn't affect interstate commerce were protected against federal interference.

But in 1954 the Supreme Court finally gave Congress the tools to fight state-sponsored segregation and racism. In *Brown v. Board of Education of Topeka, Kansas* (1954), the Supreme Court outlawed racial segregation in public schools. The decision overruled the Court's earlier "separate but equal" decision in *Plessy v. Ferguson.* In *Brown,* the Court found that "separate but equal" facilities for African Americans did not meet the Fourteenth Amendment's requirement of equal protection under the law.

By interpreting the Fourteenth Amendment to guarantee equal protection under federal *and* state laws, the Court gave the federal government the *express* power to strike down discriminatory (prejudiced) state laws and practices. Tenth Amendment questions about the line between federal and state powers were no longer relevant in these cases. Throughout the 1950s and 1960s, the Supreme Court continued to strike down racial segregation laws, as well as other state laws that discriminated on the basis of race.

A New Push for States' Rights

After the Court's NLRA decisions in the mid-1930s and the *Brown* decision in 1954, it looked like the Tenth Amendment would vanish completely from Supreme Court cases. But in *National League of Cities v. Usery* (1976), the Tenth Amendment made a surprise comeback in a Supreme Court decision.

The case involved the Fair Labor Standards Act of 1938. The act was a law that set minimum wages and maximum hours for workers. In 1974, Congress amended the law to cover most state and local government employees. In other words, the federal government was not only regulating the working conditions for private employees in the states, it was now telling the state governments what to pay their own employees.

The Supreme Court struck down the changes to the law. It stated that the Tenth Amendment prevented Congress from impairing "the States' integrity or their ability to function effectively in a federal system." In other words, the federal government could not do anything that so blatantly trampled on an accepted state power, such as paying its employees. This was the first time in forty years that the Court had struck down a federal law that had been based on Commerce Clause powers.

However, the victory for the states was short-lived. In *Garcia v. San Antonio Metropolitan Transit Authority* (1985), the Court reversed its earlier decision. The Court ruled that the federal government *could* establish working conditions and wages for state government employees. The Court ruled that it was not up to the courts to limit Congress's federal commerce powers. Instead, the Supreme Court said that because the federal government was made up of representatives from the states, the states could fight federal regulations directly in Congress. Essentially, the Court left it to the voters to draw the line between the federal and state governments.

The decision in *Garcia* seemed to be a deathblow to the Tenth Amendment. If it did not contain limits to federal power that were not already found elsewhere in the Constitution, the amendment was apparently unnecessary and useless.

However, the amendment once again rose from the ashes toward the end of the twentieth century. In *United States v. Lopez* (1995), the Court struck down the Gun-Free School Zones Act. The act made it a federal crime for any person to knowingly possess a firearm within a school zone. Congress passed the act using its Commerce Clause powers. But the Court ruled that "possession of a gun in a local school zone is in no sense an economic activity that might ... affect any sort of interstate commerce."

The Court stated that such a broad interpretation of the Commerce Clause would require the Court to conclude that "there never will be a distinction between what is truly national and what is truly local. This we are unwilling to do."

At the end of the twentieth century, gun control laws were becoming increasingly state-based, although Congress tried to pass federal legislation regulating firearms.
Reproduced by permission of
The Picture Cube.

Printz v. United States (1997) also relied on Tenth Amendment principles to restrict federal powers. The Brady Handgun Violence Prevention Act was a federal law that regulated the sale of handguns. The Court struck down a part of the law that required state officers to perform background checks on prospective handgun purchasers. It ruled that the Constitution does not permit Congress to force state officers to enforce federal laws.

A Constant Reminder of Dual Sovereignty

The Tenth Amendment was created to keep the national government from unduly expanding its powers. Since the time when the amendment was ratified, the federal government has grown enormously. Major events in the nation's history have played a role in the federal government growth. Such events include the Civil War, the Great Depression, and the Civil Rights movement, along with changes in the way the Supreme Court has interpreted the Constitution.

State governments continue to be an important and powerful part of the U.S. system of government. Issues over where to draw the line between federal and state power continue to arise. For instance, in the late 1990s many states legalized marijuana for persons suffering from certain diseases. Such laws conflicted with federal laws that outlawed such uses of the drug. President Bill Clinton (1946–)vowed that the U.S. Justice Department would try these state laws in court. The Tenth Amendment may well play a role in that dispute and others.

At the very least, the Tenth Amendment serves as a reminder that the American system of government is a dual sovereignty. The federal government's powers are limited to those expressly listed or implied in the Constitution. The states may claim all other governmental powers for themselves.

For More Information

Books

Adams, Judith. *The American Heritage History of the Bill of Rights: The Tenth Amendment.* Englewood Cliffs, NJ: Silver Burdett Press, 1991.

Bryner, Gary C., and A. D. Sorensen, eds.*The Bill of Rights: A Bicentennial Assessment.* Provo, UT: Brigham Young University, 1994.

Curie, David P.*The Constitution of the United States: A Primer for the People.* Chicago: University of Chicago, 1988.

Encyclopedia of World Biography. 17 vols. Detroit: Gale Research, 1998.

Kickok, Jr., Eugene W., ed. *The Bill of Rights: Original Meaning and Current Understanding.* Charlottesville, VA: University Press of Virginia, 1991.

Monk, Linda R. *The Bill of Rights: A User's Guide.* N.p.: Close Up Publishing, 1991.

Storing, Herbert J. *The Complete Anti-Federalist.* Edited by Murray Dry. Chicago: University of Chicago Press, 1981.

West's Encyclopedia of American Law. 12 vols. St. Paul, MN: West Group, 1998.

Articles

Anastaplo, George. "Amendments to the Constitution of the United States: A Commentary." *Loyola University of Chicago Law Journal* 23 (summer 1992): 631, 726.

Calabresi, Steven G. "'The Era of Big Government Is Over.'" *Stanford Law Review* 50 (February 1998): 1015, 1019–21.

Marks, Chris. "*U.S. Term Limits, Inc. v. Thornton* and *United States v. Lopez:* The Supreme Court Resuscitates the Tenth Amendment." *University of Colorado Law Review* 68 (spring 1997): 541–60.

Mayer, David N. "Justice Clarence Thomas and the Supreme Court's Rediscovery of the Tenth Amendment." *Capital University Law Review* 25 (1996): 339–423.

McGee, Robert W. "The Theory of Secession and Emerging Democracies: A Constitutional Solution." *Stanford Journal of International Law* 28 (spring 1992): 451, 454.

Vile, John R. "Truism, Tautology or Vital Principle? The Tenth Amendment Since *United States v. Darby.*" *Cumberland Law Review* 27 (1996–97): 445–50.

Wisdom, John Minor. "Foreword: The Ever-Whirling Wheels of American Federalism." *Notre Dame Law Review* 59 (1984): 1063–78.

Web sites

FindLaw Internet Legal Resources. *U.S. Supreme Court Opinions.* [Online] http://www.findlaw.com/casecode/supreme.html (accessed on January 24, 2000).

Hamilton, Alexander, James Madison, and John Jay. *The Federalist Papers.* Edited by Clinton Rossiter. N.p., 1961.

Jennings, Peter, and Todd Brewster "American Perspectives: The Ninth Amendment." *Mighty Words.* [Online] http://www.mightywords. com/freedom (accessed on June 7, 2000).

**Tenth
Amendment**

Eleventh Amendment

The Judicial power of the United States shall not be construed to extend to any suit in law or equity, commenced or prosecuted against one of the United States by Citizens of another State, or by Citizens or Subjects of any Foreign State.

The Eleventh Amendment was the first amendment proposed and ratified after the Bill of Rights. It was created at a time when the newly formed United States was still trying to blend the separate states into one country that worked together. The Eleventh Amendment was created to resolve a problem not adequately addressed in the Constitution: what role the federal courts played in balancing the power between the federal government and state governments.

The amendment's legal language is quite technical, but it simply means that a citizen of one state cannot use the federal court system to sue the government of another state. Also, a citizen of a foreign country cannot use the United States federal courts to sue a state government. If a citizen of one state wants to bring legal action against another state's government, he or she must use the court system of that state, and the state must agree to be taken to court. Thus, a state government cannot be forced into a federal court against its will.

Origins of the Eleventh Amendment

The Eleventh Amendment is based on a concept called sovereign immunity. A sovereign is a king or a queen. The idea of sovereign immunity started in thirteenth century England when kings had to maintain their authority. Sovereign immunity protected them from private citizens taking them to court. After all, being hauled into court by a common man was beneath a king's dignity.

RATIFICATION FACTS

PROPOSED: Submitted by Congress to the states on March 4, 1794.

RATIFICATION: Ratified by the required three-fourths of states (twelve of fifteen) on February 7, 1795. Declared to be part of the Constitution on January 8, 1798.

RATIFYING STATES: New York, March 27, 1794; Rhode Island, March 31, 1794; Connecticut, May 8, 1794; New Hampshire, June 16, 1794; Massachusetts, June 26, 1794; Vermont, between October 9, 1794 and November 9, 1794; Virginia, November 18, 1794; Georgia, November 29, 1794; Kentucky, December 7, 1794; Maryland, December 26, 1794; Delaware, January 23, 1795; North Carolina, February 7, 1795.

However, the English also believed in the rights of the private citizen. The English courts made rules so that if citizens felt the king had harmed them in some way, they could go to court and ask for compensation. A great deal of American law comes from laws created in England. Some laws were created by Parliament (England's law-making branch of government), and some were created by common law. (Common law is based on traditions. It is the way things have been done for a long time.) The idea of sovereign immunity was one taken from England's common laws.

Since America had no king, the federal government considered itself the sovereign. Today, sovereign immunity is used so that citizens cannot sue their government without the government's consent. However, this is a little more complicated in the United States. The United States is a democracy, and the government represents the people. Ultimately, the people are the sovereigns.

Balancing Power in the New Government

Since the creation of the country, citizens and leaders have disagreed about how to balance the powers of the state governments with the powers of the federal government while still protecting the rights of citizens.

THE FEDERALIST

Many opinion letters were published in New York newspapers during the winter of 1787–1788. Among them were eighty-five articles published in under the pen name Publius. The Publius letters were some of the most influential documents in support of the American Constitution.

The Publius letters were written by three statesmen who were involved in creating the Constitution: Alexander Hamilton, James Madison, and John Jay. Hamilton and Madison wrote the majority of the letters, but Jay contributed five. Hamilton and Madison had been delegates to the Constitutional Convention. Jay had been the president of the Second Continental Congress in 1778 and 1779.

Alexander Hamilton, a New York lawyer, had been very active in the fight for independence. He eventually became secretary of the Treasury under President George Washington. He was also influential in forming the domestic and foreign policies of the United States.

James Madison was sometimes called the "Father of the Constitution," because in 1776 he also helped write the state constitution for his home state of Virginia. Madison served in the Virginia legislature in the mid-1780s, and served two terms as secretary of state under President Thomas Jefferson. He was later elected the fourth president of the United States.

John Jay was another New York lawyer. He had been involved in creating the new government of the United States from the beginning of

The United States was established as a federation. That is, the separate state governments agreed to come together to form one country. Americans think of the United States as a single nation. However, the alliance between the separate states was not very stable at first. In fact, much of the Constitution spells out which powers and rights belong to the individual, to the states, and to the federal government.

The Eleventh Amendment recognizes that states have the rights of sovereign governments—including immunity—even though they belong to the union. Under the doctrine of sovereign immunity, a state can be sued only if it has agreed to be sued, and only if it has broken laws of the state. Thus, the English passed on two idea's to the United States. One,

the Revolution. Jay later became the first chief justice of the Supreme Court (see sidebar).

Hamilton, Madison, and Jay wrote the Publius letters to explain the new Constitution, and to gain support for it among voters. The letters detailed the political ideas contained in the Constitution. They presented the problems facing the new republic, and posed solutions they believed the Constitution offered. The letters explained that the new Constitution proposed a strong central government. The papers also explained that the government's power would be divided between separate institutions: the presidency, the Congress, and the courts. This separation would create a strong central power, and prevent upsetting the Union in the event of arguments between the states.

The letters helped quiet the people's concerns by explaining how the Constitution would work. Some people worried that giving the republic's citizens a great deal of personal freedom would limit the government's control. They feared all the different opinions would tear the country apart. But the letters argued that the Constitution was setting up a representative form of government to handle all the different opinions. The Constitution would not make the United States a "pure" or direct democracy. Instead, elected representatives would speak for the people in the legislature. The representatives would work out compromises to accommodate all the differing opinions.

Many wondered why the framers of the Constitution had included so many checks and balances in the government. (Continued on page 222)

the state cannot be sued against its will by a citizen. Two, citizens should have some legal way to fight back if harmed by the state. Balancing between these two principles still keeps lawyers busy.

Federalism: The Basis of American Government

When the thirteen colonies formed the United States in the early to mid-1600s, the people in the colonies were very different from each other. For example, people seeking freedom to practice their religion founded Massachusetts; business people seeking new opportunities to make money founded Virginia; criminals from other countries came to the

note: no specs were supplied for box quote, is this ok?

THE FEDERALIST *(Continued)*

James Madison used the fifty-first letter to describe why it was necessary to keep any one government official or agency from getting too much power. He wrote,

> If men were angels, no government would be necessary. If angels were to govern men, neither external nor internal controls on government would be necessary. In framing a government which is to be administered by men over men, the great difficulty lies in this: you must first enable the government to control the governed; and in the next place oblige it to control itself.

The letters were later collected and published as *The Federalist*, also called *The Federalist Papers*. Thomas Jefferson declared the letters "the best commentaries on the principles of government ... ever written." Even in the twentieth century the letters are considered an excellent statement of American political ideals, and Supreme Court Justices still refer to them.

Though Hamilton and Madison worked together and wrote the Publius letters to persuade Americans to accept the new constitution, they did not always agree with each other. By the 1790s, Hamilton and Madison had joined opposing political parties. Hamilton led the Federalist Party, and Madison led the Democratic-Republican Party.

prison colony of Georgia to work off their sentences. Most of these colonies had been founded. By the time the American Revolution began in 1775, the colonies had developed their own individual governments.

After the Revolutionary War (1775–1783) ended, the leaders of the United States faced the job of creating a new government. They wanted the separate colonies to unite, but still keep their independent identities. Federalists (those in favor of a strong national government) and Anti-Federalists (those against a strong national government) argued hotly about this topic.

Federalists, or nationalists as they were known, felt a strong federal government would aid the survival of the new union. Anti-Federalists wanted the states to stay strong, and worked to limit the powers of the federal government. The men who drafted the Constitution tried to invent a new federalism that would balance the needs of the states with the powers of the national government.

Keeping everyone happy

Before the Constitutional Convention met in Philadelphia in 1787, the states were united under a very loose agreement called the Articles of Confederation. The Articles did not provide for a president, but rather a governing committee that had very little power. At first, the delegates (representatives sent to speak and act for others) only intended to change the Articles to make a stronger government for the new nation. But, as they worked and debated, they felt that a whole new document was needed. They saw the need for a new constitution that provided for a central government strong enough to hold the states together, but also allowed the states to keep their own separate governments.

The Constitution was adopted and signed by the Constitutional Convention on September 17, 1787. Afterwards, popular conventions were held in each state. Citizens talked about the new constitution, and voted to approve or reject it. This was really the start of a new government, and people were excited about it. Many published their opinions in newspapers.

Powers of the State

The event that immediately sparked the proposal of the Eleventh Amendment was a court case brought before the Supreme Court in 1793. A South Carolinian named Alexander Chisholm wanted to sue the state of Georgia. During the Revolutionary War, the state of Georgia had bought supplies from a businessman from South Carolina, but had never paid for them. The businessman was Robert Farquar, but he died. The job of handling his estate fell to Chisholm who decided to try and collect the money Georgia owed to Farquar.

The federal court system was only a few years old when Chisholm's suit started. Article III of the Constitution outlines the structure and jurisdiction of the courts. However, the federal court for the District of Georgia was not certain it had the right to hear the *Chisholm* case.

Many of the states were very nervous when Chisholm went to the Supreme Court to ask permission to try his case in federal court, because

JUSTICE JOHN JAY (1745–1829)

John Jay was the descendant of French Protestants who fled to the new world for religious freedom in the late 1600s. John Jay's family was well established in the colonies by the time he was born in New York City in 1745. He graduated from King's College (which is now called Columbia University), where he trained as a lawyer. He joined the New York Bar Association in 1768.

Young Jay was very interested in government, and in the changes that were happening in his homeland. Because he was a respected lawyer from a prosperous old New York family, his opinions were in demand in the colonies. In 1773, Jay served the colonial government of New York as a royal commissioner. In the mid-1770s, he entered national politics when he was chosen as delegate to the Continental Congress. He served in the First Continental Congress from 1774 to 1776, and in the Second Continental Congress from 1778 to 1779. In 1779, he was elected President of the Congress.

Though Jay worked throughout his life for the new nation of the United States, he was not originally in favor of independence. Like many who came from the wealthy merchant class, he favored working out a better relationship with Britain rather than breaking away. His signature is notably missing from the Declaration of Independence.

But once the Revolutionary War started, Jay supported his country. He helped to write the New York state constitution, and represented the new country as a diplomat. As a diplomat, he traveled to Spain in 1779. However, he failed to get Spain's support for the newly independent colonies.

In 1782, he went to Paris with fellow statesmen Benjamin Franklin and John Adams to negotiate the treaty that ended the Revolutionary War. The Treaty of Paris that Jay and his fellow diplomats worked out guaranteed the United States of America's independence. Britain gave up its claims on all land east of the Mississippi River, and granted the

many of them had war debts. If the federal court forced one of the states into court, perhaps it wouldn't be long before all the states lost their power. If everyone the states owed money to sued in federal court and collected, the states would soon go broke.

new nation fishing rights in the Atlantic Ocean. It was a better deal for the new United States than anyone had thought possible.

In 1789, President George Washington appointed John Jay the country's first chief justice of the Supreme Court. During his tenure as Chief Justice, Jay and the other justices had the difficult job of interpreting the Constitution. When the Court made decisions, it had to walk a fine line between upholding the authority of the young federal government, and protecting the powers of the individual states. One of Jay's most famous rulings was *Chisholm v. Georgia*. *Chisholm* led to the passage of the Eleventh Amendment.

Jay earned much respect as a chief justice, but he did upset the American public in 1795. The end of the Revolutionary War had not ended the problems between Britain and the United States. By 1795, these problems were leading to another war. The president sent Jay to England to negotiate an agreement with the king.

Jay worked out a treaty that prevented war, but what "Jay's Treaty" gave Britain made the American public very angry. People blamed Jay for betraying American interests, and some burned him in effigy (burned a dummy with his name on it to show how much they disliked him).

But Jay's bad reputation did not last. Not long after he returned from England, he was elected governor of New York without even running for the office. During his two terms as governor, Jay improved life in New York. He helped to pass anti-slavery laws, improved the treatment of state prisoners by ending such practices as flogging and locking people up for owing money, and built more modern prisons.

After his last term as governor, Jay refused President John Adams' request for him to serve again as chief justice of the Supreme Court. Instead, Jay retired from public service to his family estate in Bedford, New York. He lived there for twenty-eight more years before he died on May 17, 1829.

The Supreme Court heard Chisholm's lawyer's arguments. The state of Georgia was angry at being forced into court, and did not send a lawyer to argue their case. The state simply refused to participate. All of the other states watched carefully to see what would happen.

**Eleventh
Amendment**

The Supreme Court, under Chief Justice John Jay, ruled four to one that Chisholm could sue Georgia in federal court, even though the state was not willing to be sued. Justice James Iredell was the only judge who didn't agree with the Court's decision. Justice Iredell declared that it violated the state's sovereign immunity.

Justice James Wilson, on the other hand, firmly stated that the idea of sovereign immunity came from societies with kings and had no place in the new republic. "The pure source of equality and justice must be founded on the consent of those whose obedience they require," he said. "The Sovereign, when traced to his source, must be found in the man." Creditors quickly filed lawsuits similar to Chisholm's against the states of Georgia, Maryland, Massachusetts, New York, South Carolina, and Virginia.

A short lived victory

On February 19, 1793, the day following the *Chisholm* decision, legislators in the Senate heard the first resolution proposing an amendment to the Constitution. The new amendment assured sovereign immunity to the individual states.

Various states submitted similar resolutions to Congress for debate. By March 4, 1794, Congress had an amendment for the states to ratify. This was very fast work for the legislature. It shows how deeply many of them felt that the Court's decision to hear the case against the state of Georgia was wrong.

The amendment's immediate purpose was to overturn the Court's verdict in *Chisholm.* However, it also ensured that no federal court would be able to try a case against a state government in the future. Within a year, the states ratified the amendment. They were anxious to protect their own rights and powers. Strangely enough, the states did not let Congress know right away that they had ratified the Eleventh Amendment. The information about the ratification did not arrive at Congress until 1797. The amendment had begun its life under President George Washington, but it became law in January 1798 under President John Adams.

BUT IS IT REALLY AN AMENDMENT? The Eleventh Amendment was the first test of the young country's amending process. The interpretation of the amending process rules became a significant point of discussion during the first court case that challenged the Eleventh Amendment.

In 1798, almost immediately after the amendment became law, a private company tried to sue the state of Virginia over land ownership in the case of *Hollingsworth v. Virginia.* Virginia declared its right to sovereign immunity, but Hollingsworth's lawyers claimed that the Eleventh Amendment was not really law because President George Washington had not signed it.

They pointed to the Constitution that states the president must sign every "order, resolution, or vote" before it becomes law. This gives the executive branch of the government some control over lawmaking. However, the Constitution does not actually say that constitutional amendments must be signed. It does not specifically give the executive branch any role in amending the Constitution. Besides, President Washington had not signed any of the previous ten amendments that make up the Bill of Rights.

The Supreme Court did not accept Hollingsworth's argument. The Court decided that the amendment process had been legal and correct according to the Constitution, and simply declared that Amendments One through Eleven were all valid. National and state governments and courts have considered them valid ever since.

The Civil War left the Southern states with many problems. They had spent all of their money fighting the war and were now very poor.

Courtesy of the National Archive and Records Administration.

The Extension of the Eleventh Amendment

When the Civil War ended in 1865, state governments in the South had a whole new set of problems. During the war, they had raised money by issuing bonds. A bond is a way a government can borrow money from its citizens. Citizens buy bonds in return for a certificate saying that they paid the money. After a period of time, they get their money back with interest (money paid for the use of loaned money). Unfortunately, sometimes governments default (fail to make payment) on their bonds, and no one gets any money back.

After the Civil War, the Southern states were very poor. They had spent all of their money fighting the war, and most were deeply in debt. There was little left to pay to those who held Confederate bonds. Many Southern citizens wanted to take the states to court and force them to repay the money.

Many complicated lawsuits followed, but the Eleventh Amendment prevented most from succeeding. By the 1890s, the Supreme Court extended the meaning of the Eleventh Amendment to forbid citizens of a state from suing their own state. That had not been the original wording of the amendment, but the justices argued that state governments should not be brought into court against their will.

Extending the force of an amendment beyond the amendment's exact wording is part of the Supreme Court's job. As interpreters of the Constitution, the justices establish rules for the country that adhere to the intent of the Constitution and its amendments. The Supreme Court has continued to extend the meaning of the Eleventh Amendment over the years. As recently as 1997, the Court expanded the meaning of the Eleventh Amendment to make it more difficult to sue state-run colleges and universities.

But is it fair?

If you are thinking that it seems unfair not to be able to sue a state government if that government has harmed you or owes you money, you are not alone. Lawyers have argued and debated constantly ever since the Eleventh Amendment became law. Some insist that a state's sovereign immunity keeps states from becoming bogged down in legal suits, and frees them to govern. Others think that the idea of sovereign immunity is outdated and undemocratic. Many states have even waived their sovereign immunity, allowing citizens to bring them to court in certain situations.

Continued Challenges to the Eleventh Amendment

The Eleventh Amendment has always been a controversial piece of legis-lation, largely because of the rights it gives to the individual states. Courts, lawyers, legislators, and private citizens have debated and argued about the powers of the federal government and the powers of the states ever since the end of the Revolutionary War.

In order to prevent any one branch from getting too powerful, the Constitution set up three branches of government: the president, the Con-gress, and the courts. The United States works the same way. The federal and state governments negotiate, work together, and even argue over issues of power and authority, and this helps to keep political power in balance.

What happens if a state government breaks a federal law?

The Eleventh Amendment was brought into the limelight during the Civil Rights movement of the 1950s and 1960s. The federal government made anti-discrimination laws that were very unpopular with the state governments in the South. Sometimes the state governments did not enforce the federal laws. When this happened, the federal courts heard cases brought by individuals against state governments and their institu-tions, such as state universities.

For example, the Supreme Court ruled in *McLaurin v. Oklahoma State Regents* (1950) that the University of Oklahoma could not force black students to sit separately from white students. The Supreme Court defended their jurisdiction over this case, and ruled that the state govern-ment had violated the Fourteenth Amendment to the Constitution by allowing unequal treatment of Black Americans. (The Fourteenth Amendment, adopted in 1868 to protect the newly freed slaves, guaran-tees, among other things, equal rights and protection under the law to all U.S. citizens. Because it has been used so often to challenge the policies of state governments, the Fourteenth Amendment has been called an amendment to the Eleventh Amendment.)

Other federal laws have questioned the idea of sovereign immunity, such as minimum wage laws and patent laws. In the 1999 case of *Alden v. Maine,* a worker tried to sue the state for paying less than the federal minimum wage. The Supreme Court ruled that the state's sovereign immunity did not allow the worker to sue the state.

However, in *College Savings Bank v. Florida Prepaid Postsecondary Education Expense Board* (1998), the Florida Prepaid Postsecondary Edu-

Eleventh Amendment

cation Expense used a method of loaning money patented by the College Savings Bank. (A patent is a grant from the government that gives the inventor of a product or process the sole right to make the product or perform the process for a certain period of time.) In this case, the Court ruled that, because the Florida Prepaid Postsecondary Education Expense Board had accepted money from the federal government, it was no longer entitled to sovereign immunity, and the bank could sue the Florida board in federal court.

A Recap of the Eleventh Amendment's Importance

The American people have granted sovereignty to some areas of the federal government, some to state governments, and some to themselves. Likewise, the framers of the Constitution granted Congress the power to establish the jurisdiction of the federal court system. However, after the Supreme Court's ruling in *Chisholm v. Georgia,* Congressmen soon recognized that an amendment to the Constitution was necessary to keep the unique relationship between the federal government and the state governments in balance. Laws could be changed, but constitutional amendments were permanent.

The Eleventh Amendment granted state governments more power. It gave both the federal government and the state governments some clear power over the federal courts by proving that constitutional amendments could overturn unpopular Supreme Court decisions (like *Chisholm*). Constitutional amendments were proven effective weights in counterbalancing the power of judicial review. In turn, Supreme Court decisions gained a greater degree of acceptance as solutions to constitutional legal disputes.

The Eleventh Amendment remains the only amendment written specifically for the federal judiciary.

For More Information

Books

Eichner, James A. *Courts of Law.* New York: F. Watts, 1969.

Feinberg, Barbara Silberdick. *Constitutional Amendments.* New York: Twenty-First Century Books, 1996.

Jacobs, Clyde E. *The Eleventh Amendment and Sovereign Immunity.* Westport, CT: Greenwood Press, 1972.

Katz, William Loren. *The Constitutional Amendments.* New York: Watts, 1974.

Miller, John C. *Federalist Era, Seventeen Eighty-Nine to Eighteen-One.* New York: HarperCollins, 1960.

Morris, Richard B. *John Jay: The Nation and the Court.* New York: Holmes & Meier, Publishers, 1967.

Orth, John V. *The Judicial Power of the United States: The Eleventh Amendment in American History.* New York: Oxford University Press, 1987.

Ravitch, Diane, and Abigail Thernstrom, eds. *The Democracy Reader: Classic and Modern Speeches, Essays, Poems, Declarations, and Documents on Freedom and Human Rights Worldwide.* New York: HarperCollins, 1992.

Summer, Lila E. *The Judiciary: Laws we Live By.* Austin, TX: Raintree Steck-Vaughn, 1993.

Eleventh Amendment

Articles

Arkes, Hadley. "More Supreme than Ever: Supreme Court Decisions Involving the Eleventh Amendment." *National Review* 50, no.14 (26 July 1999): 38–41.

Bufford, Samuel L. "The Eleventh Amendment: Unfinished Judicial Business." *The Judges' Journal* 38, no.1 (winter 1999) 6–8.

Burnham, William. "Beam Me Up, There's No Intelligent Life Here: A Dialogue on the Eleventh Amendment with Lawyers from Mars." *Nebraska Law Review* 75, no. 3, (1996): 551.

Epstein, David F. "The Federalist." *Society* 24 (Nov–Dec 1986): 16–19.

Rothenberg, Tamar. "Why Historians Call James Madison the "Father of the U.S. Constitution." *Scholastic Update* 119 (1986 September 8): 9

Web sites

"Findlaw Internet Law Center Web Site." [Online] http://www.caselaw.findlaw.com/data/constitution/amendment11 (accessed on 25 June, 2000).

"Legal Information Institute Web Site, Cornell Law School" [Online] http://wwwsecure.law.cornell.edu/topics/jurisdiction.html.

Twelfth Amendment

The Electors shall meet in their respective states and vote by ballot for President and Vice-President, one of whom, at least, shall not be an inhabitant of the same state with themselves; they shall name in their ballots the person voted for as President, and in distinct ballots the person voted for as Vice-President, and they shall make distinct lists of all persons voted for as President, and of all persons voted for as Vice-President, and of the number of votes for each, which lists they shall sign and certify, and transmit sealed to the seat of government of the United States, directed to the President of the Senate;—The President of the Senate shall, in the presence of the Senate and House of Representatives, open all the certificates and the votes shall then be counted;—The person having the greatest number of votes for President, shall be the President, if such number be a majority of the whole number of Electors appointed; and if no person have such majority, then from the persons having the highest numbers not exceeding three on the list of those voted for as President, the House of Representatives shall choose immediately, by ballot, the President. But in choosing the President, the votes shall be taken by states, the representation from each state having one vote; a quorum for this purpose shall consist of a member or members from two-thirds of the states, and a majority of all the states shall be necessary to a choice. And if the House of Representatives shall not choose a President whenever the right of choice shall devolve upon them, before the fourth day of March next following, then the Vice-President shall act as President, as in the case of the death or other constitutional disability of the President.—The person having the greatest number of votes as Vice-President, shall be the Vice-President, if such number be a majority of the whole number of Electors appointed, and if no person have a majority, then from the two highest numbers on the list, the Senate shall choose the Vice-President; a quorum for the purpose shall consist of two-thirds of the whole number of Senators, and a majority of the whole number shall be necessary to a choice. But no person constitutionally ineligible to the office of President shall be eligible to that of Vice-President of the United States.

RATIFICATION FACTS

PROPOSED: Congress proposed the twelfth amendment to the states on December 9, 1803, to replace the rules for electing the president and vice president that were set out in the original third paragraph of Article II, section one of the Constitution.

RATIFICATION: The amendment was ratified on June 15, 1804, when New Hampshire became the twelfth of the seventeen states to ratify. Eventually thirteen states ratified the amendment. The amendment was rejected by the remaining four states.

RATIFYING STATES: North Carolina, December 21, 1803; Maryland, December 24, 1803; Kentucky; December 27, 1803; Ohio, December 30, 1803; Pennsylvania, January 5, 1804; Vermont, January 30, 1804; Virginia, February 3, 1804; New York, February 10, 1804; New Jersey, February 22, 1804; Rhode Island, March 12, 1804; South Carolina, May 15, 1804; Georgia, May 19, 1804; New Hampshire, June 15, 1804. The amendment was later ratified by Tennessee on July 27, 1804.

Though the Twelfth Amendment may seem uninteresting on its surface, it was created in response to one of the most dramatic presidential elections in American history—an episode that helped spark a deadly feud between two of the nation's most prominent politicians (see "The Hamilton-Burr Duel" box).

Ratified on June 15, 1804, the Twelfth Amendment changed the way the president and vice president of the United States are elected. Before the Twelfth Amendment was passed, both the president and vice president were picked from the same group of candidates, all of whom were running for president. Generally, the candidate who won the most votes became president and the second place finisher became vice president.

With the growth of political parties (organized groups of people with similar political interests) the system led to some unexpected outcomes, including the election of a president and vice president from different parties and a tie between two candidates from the same party.

The Twelfth Amendment was designed to prevent such confusing results by providing separate selection processes for president and vice president. Throughout its history, however, the election process described by the Constitution and the Twelfth Amendment has been the subject of debate and controversy.

What is the Electoral College?

To understand the Twelfth Amendment, it is necessary to understand how the president and vice president of the United States are elected.

In the summer of 1787, delegates from twelve of the thirteen United States gathered to create a new form of government for the young country. Among the many issues discussed at this Constitutional Convention (see chapter one) was the question of how the president of the country should be elected.

The delegates, sometimes referred to as the framers of the Constitution, worried that a president who was elected directly by the people might become too popular and powerful, becoming a sort of elected king. This may seem strange today, but Americans had only recently won their independence from Britain's king in the Revolutionary War (1775–83), and the framers were in no hurry to replace one monarch (a king or queen) with another.

They were also concerned that ordinary citizens might not know enough about the various candidates to make an informed decision, largely because in those days far less information was available to most people. The media consisted mainly of local newspapers, and, of course, there was no television or radio news.

Some of the delegates wanted Congress (the legislative body made up of the Senate and the House of Representatives) to elect the president. But an essential element of the emerging Constitution was the idea of a separation of powers (see chapter one) among the executive branch (headed by the president), the legislative branch (Congress), and the judicial branch (the courts).

The framers felt that allowing Congress to select the president would undermine this separation, since the president would owe his job to the legislators.

Having it both ways

The delegates settled on a system of indirect election, known as the electoral college, which did not give Congress or the people all of the power to elect the president. Under the system, described in Article II of the Constitution, every state is given a number of representatives to the electoral college equal to the number of senators and representatives it has in Congress. Since every state is entitled to two senators and at least one representative in the House of Representatives (see chapter one), each state has at least three of these special electors.

Each state's legislature (the elected body that passes laws) is allowed to decide how the electors in that state are appointed. Once the electors are chosen, they gather in their states to cast votes for president. Their votes are then sent to Congress, where they are counted and the winner is announced.

In other words, it is the *electors* who actually vote for the president of the United States.

The framers envisioned a system where these electors, selected by the state legislatures, would use their best judgment to select the two most qualified candidates to become the president and vice president.

One man, two votes?

Originally, each elector voted for two presidential candidates. In the early days of America's independence, many people were very loyal to the states they were from. To keep electors from voting only for candidates from their own state, the Constitution required each elector to vote for at least one candidate from a different state.

The candidate with the most votes in the electoral college was declared the president, as long as that candidate received votes from more than half of the electors. This is known as an electoral majority.

If, for example, there were one hundred total electors in the electoral college, each with two votes, then two hundred votes would be cast for president. In order to win the presidency, a candidate would need votes from at least fifty-one—one more than half—of the electors.

The person receiving the second largest number of votes for president would then be named vice president. This part of the process was fairly simple.

Electing a president without a majority

Several situations could complicate the matter. For example, if no candidate won an electoral majority, the House of Representatives was required to select the president from the top five candidates.

**Twelfth
Amendment**

In these special elections, each state's group of representatives was given one vote, so large states like New York and small states like New Hampshire would have the same say in selecting the president. The House was to vote until one of the five candidates won a clear majority.

The remaining candidate with the highest number of votes in the *original* electoral college vote became the vice president. (The Senate had the power to break any tie for the vice presidency.)

And the tie goes to ...

It is possible for two candidates to tie and still win votes from a majority of the electors. In the example above fifty-one votes are necessary to win. Since each of the one hundred electors has two votes, two candidates could receive votes from fifty-one or more of the electors.

If two candidates tied while winning electoral majorities, the House of Representatives voted between the two candidates until one received a majority of the states' votes and was named president. The runner-up became vice president.

While such ties might seem unlikely, it was just such a case that led to the adoption of the Twelfth Amendment.

Early Elections and Flaws in Article II

In the first and second presidential elections under the new Constitution, George Washington (1732–1799) received votes from all of the electors. No other candidate has ever duplicated this feat in the electoral college. Washington had led the country's army during the Revolutionary War and was the young nation's biggest hero.

The framers of the Constitution, including Washington, had not counted on the growth of political parties. In fact, many of them frowned on the idea of parties, fearing that they would lead to unnecessary battles for power within the government.

Washington made efforts to include people with differing views in his first cabinet (a group of high government officials appointed by the president). But it was members of that same cabinet that eventually led America's first powerful political parties.

Political opponents serve together grudgingly

When Washington decided not to seek a third term, the 1796 presidential election became a contest between two groups. Washington's vice

John Adams became the second President of the United States. Courtesy of the National Archives and Records Administration.

president, John Adams (1735–1826), and his secretary of the Treasury, Alexander Hamilton (1755–1804), led the Federalist Party. Meanwhile, Washington's secretary of state, Thomas Jefferson (1743–1826), was at the head of the opposing Republican Party (which later became the Democratic Party; for more information, see "A Brief History of American Parties" box). Generally, the Federalists favored a strong central government, while the Republicans favored strong state governments.

In that year's electoral college, Adams won seventy-one electoral votes out of 138 to become America's second president. The Federalists had hoped South Carolina politician Thomas Pinckney (1750–1828) would be elected vice president. But not all electors who had voted for Adams cast their second vote for Pinckney, and Jefferson, who won sixty-eight votes, became the new vice president.

As a result, the country's president and vice president were political opponents from different parties, a situation the framers could not have foreseen. Observers worried that this situation would make the executive branch less effective. Indeed, Vice President Jefferson often did campaign against President Adams's policies.

Over the next three years, Congress proposed several amendments to change the way the electoral college worked, but none were adopted. In 1800 the presidential election followed the same rules.

The Jefferson-Burr deadlock

Both parties were eager not to have a repetition of the 1796 election. Federalists and Republicans introduced national tickets. These tickets specified the two candidates that the party endorsed, one for president and one for vice president. Party leaders then worked to ensure that their electors voted for both of the party's candidates. This worked a little too well.

The Federalists nominated Adams for president and Thomas Pinckney's brother, Charles Pinckney (1757–1824), for vice president. The Republicans chose Jefferson as their presidential candidate and Aaron Burr (1756–1836) as their vice-presidential candidate.

Thomas Jefferson became John Adams's vice president, even though they were from separate political parties. Courtesy of the National Portrait Gallery.

The Republicans won a majority in the electoral college, but something unexpected happened. No one made sure that one Republican elector voted for someone other than Burr, and when the votes were counted, Jefferson and Burr each received seventy-three electoral votes.

A friend in need is a friend indeed

Everyone involved knew the Republicans wanted Jefferson to be president, but the Constitution clearly left it up to the House of Representatives to break the tie. Jefferson wrote to his friend James Madison (1751–1836; fourth president of the United States) that the tie "has produced great dismay and gloom on the Republican gentlemen here, and equal exultation on the Federalists."

The reason the Federalists were so happy was that they still controlled the House of Representatives. The recent election had given the Republicans a majority in the new Congress, but the new congressional terms did not begin until December 1801. Adams's presidential term, though, was due to end in March. Therefore, the current Federalist-dominated House of Representatives would choose the next president.

Some Federalists hoped to work out a deal with Burr, giving him the presidency in exchange for his loyalty to their party. Burr publicly pledged his loyalty to Jefferson, but many believed he was secretly campaigning for votes.

Ironically, the Republican Party got its way thanks partly to one of their most prominent opponents. The dedicated Federalist Hamilton was no friend of Jefferson. But he did not like or trust Burr at all. He urged Federalists in the House to support Jefferson, calling Burr a man who "has no plan but that of getting power by any means.... "

Hamilton's campaign against Burr earned him an enemy for life, but it helped Jefferson win the election. After voting thirty-five times without giving Jefferson or Burr a majority, the House finally selected Jefferson on the thirty-sixth vote—just two weeks before Adams's term as president was officially over.

A Time for Change

At this point most observers agreed the electoral college needed an overhaul. Hamilton, a Federalist, proposed requiring electors to specifically designate which of their votes was for the president and which was for the vice president.

In 1802 Congress introduced a similar proposal, nicknamed the "discrimination amendment" because electors were to discriminate, or differentiate, between presidential and vice presidential candidates. The amendment failed to pass through Congress.

But the Republicans reintroduced the amendment in 1803, hoping the states would ratify it in time for the 1804 fall elections. Congress passed the amendment on December 9, and just months later, on June 15, 1804, the states ratified the Twelfth Amendment—in plenty of time for the presidential elections that fall.

THE HAMILTON-BURR DUEL

On July 11, 1804, Alexander Hamilton and Aaron Burr faced each other from twenty paces, pistols in hand and moments from ruin. Four years earlier, the election of 1800 had led to the creation of the Twelfth Amendment. It also led these two prominent Americans down a path of destruction.

Hamilton and Burr actually had quite a bit in common. Both had been officers in the Continental Army during the Revolutionary War; both were successful lawyers in New York; and both served in the national government. Hamilton had been George Washington's secretary of the Treasury from 1787 until 1795, and Burr had served in the Senate before becoming vice president in 1800.

Hamilton, however, was a leader of the Federalist Party while Burr was an influential member of the Republican Party. Ironically, it was Hamilton's actions to help the Republican Party that agitated the feud between them.

When Thomas Jefferson and Burr tied in the 1800 electoral college vote, it fell to the Federalist-dominated House of representatives to choose one of them as the new president. Hamilton urged Federalists to support Jefferson, the Republican Party's official candidate, even though Burr seemed willing to work with the Federalists. Hamilton was not campaigning for Jefferson as much as he was campaigning against Burr, whom he publicly declared untrustworthy.

The ill will between Burr and Hamilton continued. Fearing competition from Burr, Jefferson pushed the vice president to the sidelines of the Republican Party. Looking for other opportunities, Burr ran for governor of New York in 1804, even though he had over a year of his term

Picking the president and vice president under the Twelfth Amendment

Under the terms of the Twelfth Amendment electors no longer cast two votes for president. Instead, each elector casts one vote for president and one for vice president. The amendment still requires electors to cast at least one of their votes for a candidate from a state other than their own. This is why parties never nominate candidates for president and vice president who are from the same state.

The candidate with a majority of the votes for president becomes the president. (In 1996 there 538 total electors. Half of 538 is 269, so a

as vice president left to serve. Burr ran as an Independent Republican, hoping to gain the support of New York Federalists against the main Republican candidate, Morgan Lewis.

Hamilton, however, again urged Federalists not to support the vice president, while publicly insulting Burr. And once again, Burr lost an election to a Republican rival thanks largely to the Federalist Hamilton.

His political hopes dashed, Burr sought revenge on his longtime foe, challenging Hamilton to a duel. Hamilton agreed, assuming both men would fire harmlessly over each other's heads and then leave, having both defended their honor. This was not to be. On July 11, 1804, the rivals met on the New Jersey side of the Hudson River, across from New York. When the word was given to fire, Burr raised his pistol and shot Hamilton in the stomach.

Hamilton's own gun went off harmlessly in the air. Hamilton's friends helped him back to his home in New York, but on July 12, Hamilton, one of the Founding Fathers of the United States, died at the age of forty-seven—shot by the vice president of the nation he helped create.

As public anger over the shooting grew, the vice president fled New York, where he was charged with murder. Burr wandered through the country before returning to Washington to serve out his term as vice president, despite being a wanted man. The charges against Burr were eventually dropped.

Burr would later be implicated in a plot against the U.S. government. Those charges were also dropped, and he lived to be eighty years old. But the man who had once been one of America's most powerful politicians had permanently lost the respect and admiration of his countrymen.

candidate needed a minimum of 270 votes to win an electoral majority.) The person with a majority of the votes for vice president (rather than the person with the second most votes for president) becomes vice president.

If no presidential candidate wins a majority, the House of Representatives selects the president from the top three (rather than five) presidential vote-getters. Just as they did under the old rules, each state casts a single vote until one candidate wins a clear majority.

If the House of Representatives does not select a president in time for the new term, the vice president acts as president until the House selects a president. If there is a tie in the voting for the vice president, the Senate chooses the vice president from the top two vote-getters.

The Legacy of the Twelfth Amendment

With these small changes, the Twelfth Amendment solved a number of problems. The separate ballots for president and vice president made it easy for the party with the most electors to organize and win the votes for both the presidency and the vice presidency.

Of course, this was not what the framers had in mind. They imagined the vice president being picked from a pool of candidates deemed fit for the presidency, rather than from a group of contenders specifically chosen as vice-presidential candidates. But the Twelfth Amendment reflects the reality of party politics in America. Neither of the parties wanted a situation such as the one in which President Adams was forced to serve with an uncooperative vice president (Jefferson) from another party.

The new system also limited the role of the House of Representatives in selecting the president. Under the old system, it was possible for two candidates to tie while winning an electoral majority and therefore to turn the selection over to the House. But because electors now have only one vote for president, only one candidate can win an electoral majority. This means the House only selects the president when no candidate has won a majority in the electoral college.

Critics speak out against electoral college

Despite the changes made by the Twelfth Amendment, critics of the electoral college put forth a number of arguments for changing or even abolishing the system.

When the electoral college was first established, voters had very little say in the election of the president. Voters elected their state legislature. But members of the legislature *appointed* the electors who voted for president.

Over time, states changed their rules, allowing eligible voters to vote for the electors. Now, each party runs candidates who pledge, or promise, to vote for that party's ticket. Voters then choose electors from the party they support, and the winning party's electors then vote in the electoral college.

Some people believe this system should be replaced with one in which the people vote directly for the president. They argue that under the current system, a candidate who receives the most direct votes from the people (popular votes) could lose the election in the electoral college. In fact, such "wrong-winner" results have occurred.

THE "CORRUPT BARGAIN" OF 1824. By 1824 most electors were voted in by the people. Jefferson's Republican Party had split its support between Treasury Secretary William Crawford (1772–1834) and Secretary of State John Quincy Adams (1767–1848), John Adams's grandson. Another faction (or group), calling itself the Democratic Republicans, supported General Andrew Jackson (1767–1845). Finally, Republican Speaker of the House Henry Clay (1777–1852) declared himself a candidate for president.

Jackson, Adams, and Crawford finished first, second, and third, in that order. Not surprisingly, none of the candidates in this four-way race received a majority in the electoral college. Therefore, according to the Twelfth Amendment, the House of Representatives was to break the deadlock between the top three finishers.

Clay finished fourth and was out of the running. But he urged his supporters in the House to back Adams, who then easily won the presidency. When Adams later appointed Clay as his secretary of state, people suggested the two men had struck a "corrupt bargain."

The fact that Adams won the presidency with the support of a candidate who finished fourth, while winning fewer popular or electoral votes than Jackson, led to numerous proposals to revise or replace the electoral college. Nothing came of these proposals, but four years later Jackson and his Democrats swept Adams out of office—in part because of lingering public anger over the outcome of the 1824 election.

Lincoln's plurality in 1864

In elections where there are more than two strong candidates, a candidate may win more votes than any other candidate, without winning a majority (more than half) of the popular vote, as Jackson did in 1824. For example, one hundred voters might split their votes among three candidates, giving one candidate forty votes and the other two only thirty. A candidate who wins the most votes without winning a majority is said to have a plurality.

Under the right circumstances, the winner of a plurality in the popular election can win a clear majority in the electoral college and avoid having the House of Representatives break the deadlock.

note: subheads were coded as boxhd2.

There were no specs for a box head level 2, so used boxhd3—OK?

A BRIEF HISTORY OF AMERICAN PARTIES

America's Founding Fathers were not fans of political parties. George Washington, James Madison, and other framers of the Constitution spoke openly against partisan divisions. Nonetheless, parties were a part of American politics from the very beginning, and the very first parties actually formed around members of Washington's own cabinet.

FEDERALISTS AND REPUBLICANS. Washington's vice president John Adams (1735–1826) and secretary of the Treasury Alexander Hamilton (1755–1804) were the leaders of the Federalist party, while the first president's secretary of state, Thomas Jefferson (1743–1826), was at the center of the opposing Republican Party.

Adams and the Federalists won the first contest between the parties in 1796. But Jefferson won the next election in 1800, beginning a period of Republican control that lasted twenty-eight years. The Federalists disappeared from national politics by the 1820s, but just as the first parties grew out Washington's non-partisan administration, new parties sprung from splits within the Republican Party.

DEMOCRATS, WHIGS, AND KNOW-NOTHINGS. In 1824 Republican supporters of John Quincy Adams (1767–1848), calling themselves the National Republicans, fought off a challenge by Andrew Jackson (1767–1845) and his group of Democratic-Republicans. By the time Jackson defeated Adams in 1828, his group of Republicans was known simply as the Democratic Party.

Jackson's opponents, led by former Republican Henry Clay (1777–1852), regrouped, creating the Whig Party in the 1830s, and for the next two-and-a-half decades, the Democrats and Whigs dominated national politics.

The Know-Nothings, a party that opposed new immigration into the United States, also cropped up during this period. Renamed the

This has happened a number of times in American history. Presidents such as Woodrow Wilson (in 1920) and Bill Clinton (in 1992) have won majorities in the electoral college, despite winning only a plurality of the popular vote. But because the winners of such elections have beaten their opponents, the results are not usually controversial.

American Party, the party ran former Whig president Millard Fillmore (1800–1874) as its presidential candidate in 1856, but won just one state.

NEW REPUBLICAN PARTY. A new Republican Party, unrelated to Jefferson's party, was created in 1854. Dominated by anti-slavery interests, the Republicans became popular in the northern states just before the Civil War. In 1860 Republican candidate Abraham Lincoln won a four-way presidential race over the divided Southern and Northern Democrats. Since the Civil War (1861–65), a Republican or Democrat has won every presidential election, while the two parties have dominated politics at every level of government.

THIRD-PARTY CANDIDATES. The American electoral college system requires vast organization at the state and national levels, making it hard for new parties to run a candidate for president. Some third party candidates, though, have impacted presidential elections.

After Republicans nominated President William Howard Taft (1857–1930) in 1912, former Republican president Theodore Roosevelt (1858–1919) left the party and ran as the Progressive Party candidate. The Republican split helped Democratic candidate Woodrow Wilson (1856–1924) win the election. By finishing second, though, Roosevelt became the most successful third-party candidate ever.

Alabama governor George Wallace's (1919–1998) American Independent Party candidacy in 1968 and John Anderson's run on the Liberal Party ticket in 1980, hurt Democratic candidates in those elections. But Reform Party candidate H. Ross Perot (1930–) stands as the most successful third-party candidate since Theodore Roosevelt. The Texas businessman won nearly 19 percent of the popular vote in the 1992 election. Despite his strong showing, Perot did not receive a single electoral vote, highlighting the difficulty new parties have in cracking the American electoral system.

But timing is everything. Abraham Lincoln (1809–1865) won such an election in 1860, on the eve of the American Civil War (1861–65), in which Northern and Southern states fought over issues including states' rights and slavery. In a four-way election, Lincoln (whom people in the Southern states did not support) won a majority in the electoral college with only 40 percent of the popular vote.

Though Lincoln had finished ahead of his opponents, the Southern states used his lack of a popular majority as an excuse to question the results. The Southern states refused to accept Lincoln's win, an act that eventually led the country into the Civil War.

Cleveland loses with a majority! The unit rule strikes

In 1888 incumbent president Grover Cleveland (1837–1908) won a *majority* of the popular vote and still lost the election to Benjamin Harrison (1833–1901) in the electoral college.

How could this happen? Remember, the Constitution allows the states to determine how their

In 1992, Bill Clinton won the majority in the electoral college, but only won a plurality of the popular vote. Reproduced by permission of the White House.

electors are chosen. By 1888 most of the states had established the unit rule. This "winner-take-all" system grants all of a state's electors to the party that wins the popular election in that state.

Imagine two states—one with one thousand voters who choose ten electors to the electoral college and another with only three hundred voters and three electors. Let's say Candidate A wins all three hundred popular votes in the small state, winning three electoral votes. Now assume Candidate B barely defeats Candidate A in the larger state, 501 to 499. Because of the unit rule, Candidate B would receive all ten of the big state's electors and would lead in the electoral college ten to three, even though Candidate A had nearly three hundred more popular votes overall.

In 1888, President Grover Cleveland ran for president as an incumbent and lost the election after winning the popular vote, but failing to win the electoral vote. Courtesy of the Library of Congress.

This is basically what happened in 1888. The Democrat Cleveland won lopsided victories in some states while Harrison, a Republican, won very close elections in states that had more electoral votes. The topsy-turvy result raised questions about the fairness of the electoral college and the unit rule, but once again no changes were made to the system.

Cleveland *did not* defeat Harrison four years later, becoming the only president to date to serve non-consecutive terms (terms that were not back-to-back.)

Other close elections have raised concerns that the electoral college might again elect a candidate who lost the popular vote. Most memorably, the 2000 election between Vice President Al Gore and Texas Governor George W. Bush. It took a full four weeks for the final determination to come down as to who exactly had won the presidency, and when it did, Bush had won the electoral vote, but not the popular vote. Once again, the validity of the Twelfth Amendment was called into question.

THE ELECTORAL COUNT ACT AND THE OVERTURNED ELECTION OF 1876. A different sort of problem arose in the 1876 presidential elections when New York Democrat Samuel J. Tilden (1814–1886) appeared to have defeated Republican Rutherford B. Hayes (1822–1893) of Ohio. Republicans charged that the electoral votes in three southern states had been swayed by corruption.

Twelfth Amendment

The Twelfth Amendment makes no provision for dealing with such a problem, so Congress put the issue before a fifteen-member commission made up of eight Republicans and seven Democrats. The commission voted 8 to 7 along party lines to award the disputed votes to the Republican. With the votes switched, Hayes defeated Tilden by a single vote.

There is still disagreement about who was right in this dispute. Though no change was made to the Constitution, Congress did enact the Electoral Count Act ten years later, declaring that each state is to be the final judge of its own electoral votes.

In the 1876 election, Rutherford B. Hayes charged that his opponent had swayed the southern states by corruption. Courtesy of the Library of Congress.

The Faithless Elector Argument

Another aspect of the electoral college that nags at its critics is the concept of the faithless elector. In many states voters mark a box on their ballot by the names of the candidates for president and vice president they support. Of course, this vote really goes to a group of potential electors (whose names are often not on the ballot) who have pledged to support those candidates in the electoral college.

Nothing in the Constitution or the Twelfth Amendment, however, requires electors to honor that pledge. The framers wanted electors to use their own judgment in selecting the president and vice president.

But almost from the beginning, electors were expected to vote for the candidates they had pledged to support. Nonetheless, in each of the

1796, 1820, 1948, 1956, 1960, 1968, 1972, and 1976 elections, one elector refused to vote for the candidate to whom he or she was pledged.

Some people fear that someday a large group of electors might break their pledges to alter an election's outcome. While many states require electors to honor their pledges, the penalties for not doing so are often slight or nonexistent. Only North Carolina replaces a so-called faithless elector with one who must vote in accordance with the popular vote.

Defenders of the system point out that despite the lack of rules prohibiting such changes, only eight of the more than sixteen thousand electors chosen since 1789 have broken their pledge.

Debate Over the Fairness of the Electoral College

Still, critics argue that the current system has problems. Many suggest, for example, that the unit rule is unfair, because the losing candidate in a state receives no electoral votes, even in very close elections.

Beginning with Alexander Hamilton, people have suggested dividing states into electoral districts and granting the winning candidate in each district an electoral vote, rather than awarding all of the state's electors to one candidate. By the late twentieth century, Maine and Nebraska did not use a unit rule. Instead, they distributed their electoral votes among candidates, based on the outcome of the popular vote.

Defenders of the unit rule argue that it allows for democratic elections in each state, while giving individual states more power in the electoral process. For example, if candidates in a very close race split a state's electoral votes evenly, the state has less overall impact on the outcome of the national election than if the winner receives all of the state's votes. Knowing how much is at stake in an all-or-nothing election, candidates are less likely to take any state race for granted.

Direct vote

Close elections often raise public fears that the electoral college will deadlock or select the wrong winner and encourage support for a direct election of the president.

But defenders of the electoral college counter that such direct elections might actually prove to be less democratic. Since the electoral college rewards candidates who win a large number of votes in many states, it tends to weed out candidates who appeal to only a small part of the population. But in a direct-vote system, it is possible that many candidates—each appealing to small groups of voters—might divide the popular vote into small parts. In an election among many candidates, a candidate receiving a small share of the popular vote, say 10 percent, could become president—even though 90 percent of the public had voted for other candidates.

Over the years debate has raged over the electoral college, though the arguments for and against it have changed very little. And though Congress has considered more than five hundred proposed amendments to abolish or reform the electoral college, the basic system defined by the Constitution and modified by the Twelfth Amendment remains in place to this day.

For More Information

Books

Feinberg, Barbara S. *Electing the President.* New York: Twenty-First Century Books, 1995, p. 64.

Henry, Christopher. *The Electoral College.* New York: Franklin Watts, 1994, p. 63.

Knight, Ralph. *The Burr-Hamilton Duel.* New York: Franklin Watts, Inc., 1968, p. 63.

Nardo, Don. *The U.S. Presidency.* San Diego, CA: Lucent Books, Inc., 1995, pp. 7–52.

Steins, Richard. *Our Elections.* Brookfield, CT: Milbrook Press, 1994, p. 48.

Vail, Philip. *The Great American Rascal: The Turbulent Life of Aaron Burr.* New York: Hawthorn Books, 1973, p. 243.

Web Sites

Department of Government and Economics Houston Community College Central. *Electoral College Internet Activities and Links.* [Online] http://ccollege.hccs.cc.tx.us/instru/govecon/ec.htm (accessed August 16, 1999).

Grolier Online. *Academic American Encyclopedia: Electoral College.* [Online] http://gi.grolier.com/presidents/aae/side/elecollg.html (accessed August 16, 1999).

National Archives and Records Administration. *The Electoral College Home Page.* [Online] http://www.nara.gov/fedreg/ec-hmpge.html (accessed August 16, 1999).

Politics1.com. *Directory of Political Parties.* [Online] http://www.politics1.com/parties.htm (accessed August 16, 1999).

U.S. Embassy and Information Service in Israel. *The U.S. Electoral College: A Unique Way of Voting for the President.* [Online] http://www.usis-israel.org.il/publish/elections/colindex.htm (accessed August 16, 1999).

**Twelfth
Amendment**

Thirteenth Amendment

SECTION 1. Neither slavery nor involuntary servitude, except as a punishment for crime whereof the party shall have been duly convicted, shall exist within the United States, or any place subject to their jurisdiction.

SECTION 2. Congress shall have power to enforce this article by appropriate legislation.

The drafting of the Thirteenth Amendment was a direct result of the North's victory in the Civil War, which ended the longstanding slavery controversy. The Thirteenth became the first of three amendments passed after the Civil War between 1865 and 1870. Known as the Civil War amendments, they focus on protecting individual rights and raising the legal status of black Americans to that enjoyed by whites.

The amendment's primary goal was to end the master-slave relationship. Slavery had long been a cornerstone of the U.S. economy since colonial days, providing a cheap labor force for the expanding agricultural region of the South. Originally shipped from Africa, the slave population had increased dramatically. A growing abolitionist (people wanting to end slavery) movement in the North led to increased sectional division between the North and South. The lack of resolution of the slavery issue by Congress or the courts led ultimately to the Civil War and resolution on the battlefield.

The amendment is very brief, composed of two sections. Section 1 directly prohibits slavery and most other forms of involuntary servitude where people are forced to work for others against their will. Section 2 gives Congress power to pass laws aggressively enforcing section 1.

Differing legal interpretations of the brief amendment arose immediately. Some argued the amendment was only intended to legally resolve the

RATIFICATION FACTS

PROPOSED: Submitted by Congress to the states on January 31, 1865.

RATIFICATION: Ratified by the required three-fourths of states (twenty-seven of the thirty-six states) on December 18, 1865.

RATIFYING STATES: Illinois, February 1, 1865; Rhode Island, February 2, 1865; Michigan, February 2, 1865; Maryland, February 3, 1865; New York, February 3, 1865; Pennsylvania, February 3, 1865; West Virginia, February 3, 1865; Missouri, February 6, 1865; Maine, February 7, 1865; Kansas, February 7, 1865; Massachusetts, February 7, 1865; Virginia, February 9, 1865; Ohio, February 10, 1865; Indiana, February 13, 1865; Nevada, February 16, 1865; Louisiana, February 17, 1865; Minnesota, February 23, 1865; Wisconsin, February 24, 1865; Vermont, March 9, 1865; Tennessee, April 7, 1865; Arkansas, April 14, 1865; Connecticut, May 4, 1865; New Hampshire, July 1, 1865; South Carolina, November 13, 1865; Alabama, December 2, 1865; North Carolina, December 4, 1865; Georgia, December 6, 1865.

black slavery issue. This interpretation would allow states to address other issues related to involuntary servitude, such as peonage, on their own, free from federal government involvement. Peonage is when a person is forced against his or her will to work for another to pay off a debt. However, others contended the amendment should be interpreted much more broadly, addressing a more general concept of freedom. They asserted that only Congress, and not the states, could determine the full extent and meaning of involuntary servitude in section 1 and under section 2 pass all laws needed to ensure citizens were not subjected to that servitude. The second interpretation is the one the U.S. Supreme Court ultimately accepted.

Origins of the Thirteenth Amendment

The shipping of black slaves from Africa to the American colonies began in the late 1600s. By the time of the American Revolution (1775–1783), more than five hundred thousand black slaves were in the colonies, predominantly in the South.

Thirteenth Amendment

Slavery was a key to the new nation's struggling economy, primarily in the agricultural South. Like Thomas Jefferson, who drafted the Declaration of Independence in 1776, many of the framers to the Constitution were slaveholders. Consequently, the 1787 document made no direct mention of slavery. In fact, protection was provided to Southern slaveholding states in several clauses. The three-fifths clause gave slave states representation in Congress based on 60 percent of their slaves. Two clauses limited taxation on slaves. The Constitution also prohibited Congress from outlawing the bustling African slave trade until 1808. Another clause required the return of fugitive slaves to their owners. Federal troops could also be used to suppress slave rebellions. The Constitution essentially protected slavery in any state where citizens wanted it.

Like many during the time, Thomas Jefferson was a slaveholder. Courtesty of the National Archives and Records Administration.

Americans increasingly saw slavery as inhumane and inconsistent with the concepts of freedom and liberty. Consequently, the political and legal conflict over slavery escalated in the United States up through the mid-nineteenth century. However, it was generally accepted through this time that the national government had no authority to interfere with slavery where it existed. Meanwhile, the United States was experiencing dramatic growth economically, geographically, and politically. But the nation's Northern and Southern states progressed along vastly different paths. The North's economy became increasingly industrial while the South's economy remained predominately agricultural. Improvements in cotton fiber processing propelled a cotton production boom in the early nineteenth century. The cotton industry spread rapidly from South Carolina to Texas. More slaves were needed to keep up with the cotton demand.

While professing to be a champion of freedom to the world, the United States had become the world's largest slaveholding nation. Many citizens found this trend shameful. Since the ratification process requires three-fourths of the states to approve a new amendment, the slaveholding states always had a sufficient number to readily block any amendment designed to change the Constitution and restrict slavery.

Events escalate tension

A number of major events in the nation's growth during the early nineteenth century served to escalate tensions between the North and South. New western territories requesting statehood threatened the fragile balance of power in Congress between free states and slavery states. In an effort to maintain an equal number of slave and free states, Congress adopted the Missouri Compromise in 1820. The compromise allowed the practice of slavery to expand to some western U.S. territories but not to others. However, the Supreme Court ruled the compromise unconstitutional, once again raising fears of an uncontrolled spread of slavery in the West. The issue of expanding slavery dominated politics in the 1850s.

Though few in number, the larger plantations ruled Southern life with the owners living like European nobility. A way of life dependent on cheap, slave labor had become entrenched in the South. With the growing antislavery movement in the North, Southern leaders feared the federal government would apply increased pressure to force substantial changes in the South's economy and society. This prospect of federal intervention was highly unacceptable to the Southern leaders who strongly supported states' rights (freedom of states from federal government control). Slavery thus also became the major states' rights issue of the mid-nineteenth century.

Significantly adding to the escalating volatility was the Fugitive Slave Law passed by Congress in 1850 and the Supreme Court's *Dred Scott* decision in 1857. The law made it a crime for citizens not to help catch and return slaves who had fled the South. This requirement was very unpopular among many Northerners who sympathized with those slaves seeking freedom. The *Dred Scott* ruling held that Congress did not have authority under the Constitution to abolish slavery. In addition, slaves were not considered citizens, but rather a form of property. The Court, therefore, left it to others to resolve the bitter controversy, either politically or on the battlefield.

Abraham Lincoln and war

In 1850, neither of the two main political parties in the United States, the Democrats and the Whigs, was willing to take a strong antislavery stance. Those firmly opposed to slavery grew disillusioned with the two parties and formed the Republican Party in 1854. While most Republicans were primarily interested in stopping the spread of

Abraham Lincoln was elected president, even though the South knew that he was against slavery. Reproduced by permission of the Corbis Corporation.

slavery to new states and territories, some were abolitionists and opposed to slavery anywhere in the nation, even the South. The party quickly made a strong showing winning a third of the popular vote in the 1856 presidential race.

Four years later, the Republican Party nominated Abraham Lincoln (1809–1865) of Illinois as their presidential candidate. The South perceived Lincoln as anti-states' rights and antislavery though Lincoln publicly professed a middle course.

Fearing federal government interference with the Southern traditional way of life, including slavery, the election of Lincoln triggered a rapid sequence of Southern states seceding from the Union. Even before he took office, South Carolina seceded (formally left the Union) on December 20, 1860, followed by Mississippi, Florida, Alabama, Georgia, Louisiana, and Texas during the next several weeks. In an effort to limit the number of states seceding and avoid conflict, in his March 4 inaugural address Lincoln proclaimed, "I have no purpose directly or indirectly to interfere with the institution of slavery in the States where it exists."

The seccession of Southern states from the United States in 1860 and 1861 significantly altered congressional politics. The free states suddenly held almost total control in Congress.

With war under way, Lincoln devised a clever plan to address slavery. He could legally seize any property the enemy (the South) used to wage war against the United States. Black slaves, deemed "property" by the Supreme Court in *Dred Scott,* raised food and cotton fiber for the Southern war effort and served as laborers and teamsters in the Confederate army. Lincoln reasoned that because slaves were property and were being used to wage war against the United States, he could rightfully seize the slaves when given the opportunity. Hence, when three slaves escaped to Union lines in May 1861, the local Union commander refused to return them. Soon hundreds of other slaves escaped to Union lines. In

Thirteenth Amendment

Slaves continued to toil in the South after slaves were freed in the North.
Courtesy of the Library of Congress.

March 1862, Congress passed a law forbidding Union officers to return fugitive slaves. Increasing numbers of slaves fled in 1862.

The Emancipation Proclamation

Lincoln faced increasing public pressure to proclaim emancipation (freedom) for the slaves. Before long, the use of emancipation to weaken the South's war effort by freeing the slaves became more attractive. In July 1862, Congress passed two laws, a confiscation act freeing slaves from owners who actively supported the Confederacy and a militia act giving Lincoln power to use freed slaves in the Union army.

Soon, Lincoln boldly decided to go even further than Congress. He decided to issue a proclamation freeing all slaves in states waging war against the United States. In an effort to gain support of conservatives in the North who supported slavery, Lincoln argued that freeing slaves was the only way to win the war. Lincoln assured them that if he could save the Union without freeing slaves, he would. But, in September 1862, Lincoln warned all states at war with the Union: on January 1, 1863, their slaves would be free.

Many freed black Americans fought for the North in the Civil War. Reproduced by permission of AP/Wide World Photos.

True to his word, on January 1, Lincoln issued the historic Emancipation Proclamation, formally committing U.S. troops to liberate slaves in the Confederate states. The Civil War, largely begun over the issue of states' rights became more openly a war over slavery. The proclamation was limited in scope. It did not free slaves in the border slave states that had stayed with the Union. Lincoln tried to persuade these border states to voluntarily free slaves, even offering federal compensation (payment) to slaveholders, but none took the offer. The proclamation did not affect parts of three Confederate states as well that were under Union military control at the time. In keeping with the congressional acts passed in 1862, the Emancipation Proclamation also authorized use of freed slaves and free blacks as Union soldiers. As a result of the proclamation, 180,000 freed black Americans fought in the Union army and 10,000 in the navy.

A new amendment

Nearing the end of the Civil War, Lincoln and others believed the Emancipation Proclamation was basically a war measure that would have no constitutional legality during peacetime. Considerable doubt existed over Lincoln's power to have issued the proclamation in the first place and similarly, a general belief existed that Congress had no power to pass laws supporting emancipation. Slavery likely would once again be restored in the South. A constitutional amendment to abolish slavery was needed.

The Senate, overwhelmingly controlled by antislavery Republicans, readily passed the proposed Thirteenth Amendment on April 8, 1864. However, with a larger proportion of pro-slavery Democrats in the House, the amendment could not gain passage at first, and a lengthy political battle developed. In the 1864 fall elections, the Republicans gained more seats in the House, and the amendment consequently passed on January 31, 1865. Next loomed the difficult state ratification process (three-fourths of the states must approve amendments). The federal government required the Southern states to ratify the amendment before they could be readmitted into the Union. It took almost another eleven months before the three-fourths approval by the states was achieved.

The Thirteenth Amendment and the Supreme Court

Before adoption of the Thirteenth Amendment, five basic categories of slavery cases had come before the Supreme Court: African slave trade;

**Thirteenth
Amendment**

interstate commerce (conducting business across state boundaries) and slavery; return of fugitive slaves; slavery in the western territories; and, travel of slaves through free states. The pro-slavery perspectives of chief justices John Marshall (1755–1835) and Roger Brooke Taney (1777–1864) were influential. Throughout the history of the Supreme Court, until the Civil War, most court justices were Southerners. Most of the Northerners on the Court were Democrats who sympathized with the pro-slavery South. Except for some early slave trade cases, most important slavery cases came before the Court when Taney, an ardent slavery supporter, was chief justice. The Court's decisions from 1837 until the Civil War reflected this pro-slavery slant.

The court interprets the slavery amendment

The amendment introduced a radically new legal concept to the nation. It marked the first time federal law placed a restriction on the power of states to define the status of their own residents. Following the Civil War, abolitionist chief justice Salmon P. Chase (1808–1873) led the Court. But the Court's support of the amendment did not come easily. The Court would have to build a new legal philosophy based on concepts of freedom and racial equality. This transition in the Court's perspective proved difficult and slow, often resulting in rulings that did little to protect the newly established freedoms.

Section 1: Prohibition of Slavery and Involuntary Servitude

Congress's intent with passage of the Thirteenth Amendment was to take the question of emancipation out of the nation's politics and relieve sectional strife between the North and South. Section 1 directly prohibited slavery and involuntary servitude. The primary concern was the scope of the definition of involuntary servitude. Two main factors are involved in involuntary servitude: (1) the involuntary nature of the labor, having to act against one's will; and, (2) servitude that is the labor of one individual being fully controlled by another person. Section 1 clearly stated that being legally imprisoned for a crime is not involuntary servitude.

Was involuntary servitude concerned only with black slavery, or did it have a broader meaning? As early as 1873, in the *Slaughter-House Cases,* the Supreme Court observed that the word servitude had a larger meaning than just slavery, although "the obvious purpose was to forbid all shades and conditions of African slavery." The Court had to consider whether the amendment gave protection to persons not of African descent. The resulting *Slaughter-House* decision revealed an evolving interpretation of section 1 that would include individuals with ancestry other than black and would give early acknowledgement that peonage (when a person is forced to work for another to pay off a debt) was a form of involuntary servitude. The court stated that although "Negro slavery alone was in the mind of the Congress which proposed the thirteenth article [amendment], it forbids any other kind of slavery, now or hereafter. If Mexican peonage or the Chinese coolie labor system shall develop slavery of the Mexican or Chinese race within our territory, this amendment may safely be trusted to make it void."

A few years later in the *Civil Rights Cases* (1883), the Court observed that the amendment was "self-executing," meaning it abolished slavery and "established universal freedom" without the need of further congressional legislation to make slavery illegal.

Uncertain freedom

In legal processes, the Court's interpretation of slavery being illegal largely remained noncontroversial through the years. But in practice, as slaves throughout the South took their first cautious steps as freed people, the South's reaction to the Thirteenth Amendment was hostile. Opposition to ending slavery remained strong, and many whites refused to treat freed slaves equally. From state to state in the South, new laws known as the Black Codes were enacted from 1865 to 1866. The various codes were meant to keep blacks from being free and tried to bring back slavery in all but name. Realizing the former slaves' liberty was insecure, Congress turned to section 2 of the amendment.

Section 2: Enforcement by Appropriate Legislation

Section 2 gave Congress power to pass laws enforcing section 1 where it saw the need. The other two Civil War amendments, the Fourteenth (ratified in 1868) and the Fifteenth (ratified in 1870), also ended with sections giving Congress power to enforce the amendments with appropriate legislation. The extent of Congress's enforcement powers was immediately called into question. Was Congress empowered to pass laws dealing only with very narrow topics such as black slavery or with broad issues such as various forms of discrimination?

Enforcement acts of Congress

Congress decided it could indeed pass legislation dealing with many equality issues. One of the first pieces of legislation it passed was the Civil Rights Act of 1866. The act attempted to enforce the ban on slavery by securing "to all citizens of every race and color, and without regard to previous servitude, those fundamental rights which are the essence of civil freedom, namely the same right to make and enforce contracts, to sue, ... give evidence, and to inherit, purchase, lease, sell, hold and convey [transfer to another] property, as enjoyed by white citizens."

Another act, the Peonage Abolition Act of 1867, declared unlawful "the holding of any person to service or labor under the system known as peonage." It nullified "all acts, laws, resolutions, or usages" that maintained a system of peonage.

Nine years later, the Civil Rights Act of 1875 was passed. The first section of the act addressed the problem of discrimination (giving privileges to one group but not to another similar group) in public accommodations. Although it might be privately owned, an accommodation is considered public if its facilities are available to the general population. Examples are inns, theaters, restaurants, railroad cars — all facilities former slaves were routinely being denied use of.

The denial of equal access to such accommodations and various other discriminatory situations including denial of property ownership to blacks collectively became known as "badges of slavery." Although not specifically slavery, they resulted in unequal access and treatment, effectively keeping blacks in a subservient (suppressed) condition.

Enforcement powers come crumbling down

Early lower court rulings and a Supreme Court dissenting opinion in *Blyew v. United States* (1871) hinted the courts might support broad congressional powers of enacting laws to enforce the Civil War Amendments. But this viewpoint began crumbling with the Supreme Court case, the *Civil Rights Cases* (1883). Limitation of Congressional powers continued with *Plessy v. Ferguson* (1896) and peaked with *Hodges v. United States* in 1906. The question of peonage produced its own set of court cases that also began at the beginning of the twentieth century.

Civil Rights Cases

The *Civil Rights Cases* (1883) came to the Supreme Court as a direct challenge to the constitutionality of the Civil Rights Act of 1875.

To be constitutional, a law passed by Congress must reflect what the U.S. Constitution and its amendments intended. The case was a combination of five cases gathered together into one case. The cases all involved black individuals being denied access to accommodations — privately owned hotels, theaters, and a railway car.

In its decision, the Court reaffirmed that Congress was empowered to pass laws to abolish badges of slavery. However, the Court viewed badges to be along the lines of those rights listed in the Civil Rights Act of 1866. Writing for the Court, Justice Joseph Bradley (1813–1892) refused to view racial discrimination such as refusal of accommodations at an inn or theater as any manner of servitude or form of slavery. In a famous quote, Bradley observed, "It would be running the slavery argument into the ground, to make it apply to every act of discrimination which a person may see fit to make as to the guests he will entertain, or as to the people he will take into his coach or cab or car, or admit to his concert or theater." Therefore, Bradley rejected the 1875 act based on the Thirteenth Amendment. The amendment only authorized Congress to pass legislation to ban forms of slavery, and refusal of accommodations was not a "badge of slavery."

Bradley also struck down the act using the Fourteenth Amendment by declaring the Fourteenth prohibited discriminatory actions by a state but not discrimination by private individuals.

With the ruling, black Americans lost all five cases making up the *Civil Rights Cases*. However, it is important to note that although the Supreme Court had struck down the Civil Rights Act of 1875, it had not invalidated the Civil Rights Act of 1866.

Many Southern states took advantage of the *Civil Rights Cases* decision by passing laws that enforced racial segregation (keeping races separated) and discrimination in public places. These laws were known as the Jim Crow Laws. The court approved these laws in 1896.

Plessy v. Ferguson

In *Plessy v. Ferguson* (1896) the Supreme Court gave approval to the Jim Crow laws when it upheld as constitutional segregation on railroad passenger cars. The court ruled that such racial segregation did not violate the Thirteenth Amendment because no condition of involuntary servitude was established. In the lone dissent in the case, Justice John Marshall Harlan (1833–1911) argued that "separation of citizens, on the basis of race, while they are on a public highway, is a badge of servitude

RACIAL HOUSING RESTRICTIONS AS BADGES OF SLAVERY

Only a year after adoption of the Thirteenth Amendment, Congress passed the Civil Rights Act of 1866, which directed that "citizens of every race and color" would have "the same right ... [to] purchase, lease, sell, hold, and convey [transfer to another] ... property ... as is enjoyed by white citizens."

Nevertheless, by the 1910s, voluntary agreements among white residents, known as restrictive covenants, were established banning residents of particular neighborhoods from selling or renting their homes to blacks. These became common in the newly flourishing suburban residential developments of the 1960s.

In 1965, a black American, Joseph Lee Jones, wished to purchase a home in the newly established Paddock Woods subdivision in a suburb of St. Louis, Missouri. The developer, Alfred H. Mayer Company, indicated to Jones that it was their policy not to sell to blacks. In reaction to Mayer's policy, Jones promptly filed a lawsuit with the District Court of the Eastern District of Missouri, claiming that refusal to sell a house to a person solely because he is black violated the 1866 Civil Rights Act. Jones requested an injunctive order to force Mayer to abandon its policy and sought monetary damages for the humiliation the policy caused. Both the district court and later the appeals court dismissed Jones's suit by ruling that the 1866 act's prohibitions applied only to government actions. Mayer Company was privately owned and not subject to the act's restrictions. Jones took his case to the U.S. Supreme Court.

The court largely focused on what Congress intended when it passed the 1866 act. Were the antidiscrimination prohibitions intended to apply to everyone, or only governments? The resulting decision held that the act applied to everyone. Justice Potter Stewart, after examining historic records of the congressional debates leading to the act's passage and aware of private hostility that blacks faced at that time,

wholly inconsistent with the civil freedom and the equality before the law established by the constitution." With the *Plessy* decision, the separate but equal doctrine was established. Facilities for blacks could be separate from white facilities as long as the blacks' facilities were equal

declared that the act seemed plainly written to prohibit all racial dis-crimination regardless of whether a governmental action or by private people. The Court ruled that the refusal of the Mayer Company to sell Jones a house solely because he was black violated his civil rights and that he was entitled to payment of damages.

The Court further emphasized that the Thirteenth Amendment prohibiting slavery had given Congress the authority it needed for "abolishing all badges and incidents of slavery in the United States" and that unfair housing practices were indeed "incidents of slavery." If certain civil rights considered essential for freedom were denied, then the court could consider it a form of slavery.

Stewart wrote: "Surely Congress has the power under the Thir-teenth Amendment rationally to determine what are the badges and the incidents of slavery, and the authority to translate that determination into effective legislation ... Just as the Black Codes, enacted after the Civil War to restrict the free exercise of those rights were substitutes for the slave system, so the exclusion of Negroes from white communities became a substitute for the Black Codes. And when racial discrimina-tion herds men into ghettos and makes their ability to buy property turn to the color of their skin, then it too is a relic of slavery ... At the very least, the freedom that Congress is empowered to secure under the Thirteenth Amendment includes the freedom to buy whatever a white man can buy, the right to live where a white man can live. If Congress cannot say that being a free man means at least that much, then the Thirteenth Amendment made a promise the Nation cannot keep."

In delivering its decision, the Court had recognized that many laws and widespread social customs of the early twentieth century had kept black Americans in a situation not resembling freedom. The Court's deci-sion in *Jones* was an important influence on later civil rights legislation as well as supporting fairness in housing. Congress had power under the Thirteenth Amendment to prohibit racial discrimination by private indi-viduals as well as discrimination resulting from government actions.

or as good as the whites'. In reality, blacks' facilities such as schools, hotels, and public transportation vehicles always fell far short of white facilities. With the separate but equal doctrine, civil rights laws passed by Congress were ignored.

Hodges v. United States

The lessening of congressional powers under the Thirteenth's section 2 to pass laws protecting blacks from racial discrimination had begun in *Civil Rights Cases* and reached a new low in *Hodges v. United States* (1906). The Court ruled that the federal government had no authority to prosecute a gang of white citizens who forced blacks off a job in Arkansas because this was private discrimination and not discrimination by any government. It was strictly an action by private individuals, and private discrimination could not constitutionally fall under the civil rights laws.

PEONAGE. Violations of the Peonage Abolition Act of 1867, a law passed under section 2 of the Thirteenth Amendment, did not become a serious concern of the U.S. Justice Department until after 1900. With little controversy, the court had acknowledged peonage as a form of involuntary servitude in the *Slaughter-House Cases* (1873). But peonage was established in many southern states through a system of state laws and customs. It was a cornerstone that permitted prosecution of laborers who tried to abandon their jobs. The majority of victims of peonage laws were black Americans. In *Clyatt v. United States* (1905) Samuel Clyatt tested the legality of forcing a person in debt to labor under contract until the debt could be paid off. Citing the 1867 Peonage Act, the Supreme Court decided in Clyatt's favor.

During the same period, U.S. District Judge Thomas Goode Jones heard multiple peonage cases, the *Alabama Peonage Cases,* and struck down several Alabama laws. Jones affirmed the right of an individual to work where he or she pleases and that debt collection is generally subject to civil suits under contract law, but not to criminal proceedings. The threat of criminal proceedings had previously coerced people to stay under forced labor. Jones's efforts led to Supreme Court decisions in *Bailey v. Alabama* (1911) and *United States v. Reynolds* (1914), together called the *Peonage Cases.* In *Bailey* the Court ruled that a state "may not compel one man to labor for another in payment of a debt by punishing him as a criminal if he does not perform the service or pay the debt." The decisions, based on the 1867 act, knocked out support of the southern peonage system, which was seen as one of the last remnants of slavery.

A NON-FACTOR IN LAW. With the exception of the peonage issue, the Thirteenth Amendment became a non-factor in law. But why were there such adverse rulings undercutting the Thirteenth Amendment's effectiveness in fighting racial discrimination? Some legal scholars have pointed to a variety of factors existing in the late nineteenth century. One was that the public had likely grown weary of attempts to force social change on the South. Another major factor was that a general insensitivity to individual rights clearly persisted during this period. Individual rights were more associated with the opportunity to make a living, not civil rights.

Return of the Thirteenth

For sixty years, states enforced racial segregation in many public places, including public schools, transportation, and numerous other aspects of everyday life. A number of cases came to the Court claiming private covenants (agreements) used among whites to not sell or lease property to blacks violated the Thirteenth Amendment. But the Court refused to hear such claims, allowing the covenants to stand.

Finally, fundamental changes in law came in 1954 with the historic *Brown v. Board of Education of Topeka, Kansas* decision, which overturned *Plessy* and outlawed the separate but equal doctrine. But the successful arguments for striking down segregation in public schools was

Labor under threat of violence or physical restraint is also considered involuntary servitude by the Thirteenth Amendment.

Reproduced by permission of AP/Wide World Photos.

MILITARY DUTY

The drafting of young men into required military service has a long history of controversy in the United States, beginning with the Revolutionary War (1775–1783) when the colonies denied the creation of a national army. The U.S. Constitution, adopted in 1789, gave Congress the "power to raise and support armies" but did not address power to draft people into service. Not until the American Civil War (1861–1865) did Congress pass a draft law, the Union Draft Law of 1863, making every male citizen between twenty and forty-five years of age subject to the draft. The principle behind draft laws is that in a democracy when the security of a nation is in danger, every citizen has the duty to serve his country.

The 1863 law allowed draftees to hire a substitute or pay $300, roughly equal to a worker's yearly wages, to escape service. The unpopular law, which allowed the wealthy to buy their way out, led to draft riots across the country in 1863. Although highly controversial, the Civil War draft law was never legally tested in the Supreme Court. The legality of a national draft remained unchallenged.

When America entered World War I (1914–18)in February 1917, the nation immediately faced the problem of how to quickly assemble a large army. In May 1917, Congress passed the Selective Service Act, which required young men between ages twenty-one and thirty to register with the government so that they could potentially be selected for required military service. This time, substitutes and pays-offs were prohibited though it did allow for some exemptions.

based on the Fourteenth Amendment's equal protection clause, not the Thirteenth Amendment. In 1964 Congress passed the most comprehensive civil rights legislation since the 1875 act. The Civil Rights Act of 1964 was largely based on the commerce clause in Article I of the Constitution, not the Thirteenth Amendment. Four years later, in 1968 the Thirteenth Amendment finally made a dramatic comeback in the courtroom in *Jones v. Alfred H. Mayer Company.*

In making the far-reaching *Jones* ruling, the Court first had to establish whether Congress had the power to enact the Civil Rights Act of 1866. The Court had never invalidated this act as it had the Civil Rights Act of 1875. It was clear to Justice Potter Stewart (1915–1985)

Although twenty-four million men complied with the act and registered for the draft, more than two million did not. Additionally, almost 340,000 failed to report when called or deserted after arrival at training camp. The U.S. government arrested many who avoided military service, and some of those arrested legally challenged the draft law. The Supreme Court combined several cases challenging the draft into one case known as the *Selective Draft Law Cases*. The resisters argued that the Constitution did not give Congress power to command men to serve in the military against their will. As part of their argument, they claimed the draft was a form of involuntary servitude prohibited by the Thirteenth Amendment.

A unanimous Court rejected all of the resisters' arguments in upholding the Selective Service Act. The court ruled that not only did the Constitution give Congress power "to raise and support armies" and "make all laws which shall be necessary and proper" to carry out that power, but that they saw no similarity between what the Thirteenth Amendment called involuntary servitude and military service. The Court ruled citizenship carried with it an obligation to perform the "supreme and noble duty of contributing to the defense of the rights and honor of the nation as the result of a war declared by the great representative body of the people." This obligation does not violate prohibitions of the Thirteenth Amendment. Use of the military draft ended in 1973 as the Vietnam War neared an end, but required registration continued to the end of the twentieth century in order to maintain a list of men in case a need suddenly arises.

that section 2 of the Thirteenth Amendment was all the authority needed to pass the act abolishing badges of slavery, in this case a private developer refusing to sell a home to a black man. The amendment, Stewart also reasoned, provided constitutional support for congressional legislation against private racial discrimination.

At last with the *Jones* decision, Congress had the constitutional support of section 2 of the Thirteenth Amendment to enact laws prohibiting racial discrimination. Other cases followed on the heels of *Jones*. In *Sullivan v. Little Hunting Park* (1969) the Court ruled the 1866 act protects a black resident's share in a neighborhood recreational club that normally was available with the lease or purchase of a house in an area.

Johnson v. Railway Express Agency (1975) supported federal remedies for racial discrimination in private employment. In *Runyon v. McCrary* (1976) the Court ruled that all people have the right to make and enforce contracts and that black children have the right to attend commercially operated private nonsectarian schools (not sponsored by a religious denomination). In essence, the 1866 act could apply to all areas that Congress has authority, including school segregation.

Thirteenth Amendment issues continue

Cases near the end of the twentieth century involved issues other than racial discrimination and further examined the meaning of involuntary servitude. *United States v. Kozminski* (1988) involved two mentally retarded men in poor health who worked seventeen hours a day for seven days a week for little pay. Employers applied various physical and psychological threats. The Court held that "the term 'involuntary servitude' necessarily means a condition of servitude in which the victim is forced to work for the defendant through use of or threat of physical restraint or physical injury, or by the threat of coercion through the legal process." Involuntary servitude cannot involve psychological coercion alone. Some physical or legal coercion must be present.

Another form of involuntary servitude could include religious sect (organized group) activities. In several cases in the 1980s, courts have ruled that religious sects may be found guilty of involuntary servitude if an individual is clearly being held against his or her will.

Situations where the Thirteenth does not apply

Through time the Court has also identified certain legal requirements of citizens, including civic responsibilities, which are not considered involuntary servitude. In *Robertson v. Baldwin* (1897) the Court ruled that seamen may have to give up some personal liberties through the contracts they sign. The resulting work on the high seas subject to the commands of the ship's captain is not involuntary servitude. The Thirteenth Amendment protections also do not apply to the military draft as determined in *Selective Draft Law Cases* (1918) and later reaffirmed in *United States v. O'Brien* (1968). In 1911 the Court upheld that convicts can be required to work on public street projects as part of their sentence and that the government can also collect overdue taxes or child support from workers' wages. Also, a state can require people to obtain employment as a condition of participating in public assistance programs. Student requirements of community service for graduation also did not constitute involuntary servitude or peonage. The court held in *UAW v. WERB* (1949) that injunctions and cease and desist orders in labor disputes requiring workers to return to work do not violate the Thirteenth Amendment. Other civic duties that do not violate the Thirteenth Amendment includes requirements to serve on grand juries as decided in *Hurtado v. United States* (1973).

Summing the Parts of the Thirteenth Amendment

Taken together and integrated at the beginning of the twenty-first century in light of more than one hundred years of court decisions, the Thirteenth Amendment banned slavery and other forms of involuntary servitude and gave Congress the power to pass laws to carry out the bans. Although abolishing African slavery was the initial goal, the Thirteenth allows Congress to pass laws prohibiting many forms of racial discrimination, regardless of whether imposed by a private individual or by government.

For More Information

Books

Buchanan, G. Sidney. *The Quest for Freedom: A Legal History of the Thirteenth Amendment.* Houston: Houston Law Review, 1976.

Finkelman, Paul. *Slavery and the Founders: Race and Liberty in the Age of Jefferson.* Armonk, NY: M. E. Sharpe, 1996.

Finkelman, Paul, ed. *Slavery and the Law.* Madison, WI: Madison House, 1996.

Hall, Kermit L., ed. *The Law of American Slavery: Major Historical Interpretations.* New York: Garland Publishers, 1987.

Hoemann, George H. *What God Hath Wrought: The Embodiment of Freedom in the Thirteenth Amendment.* New York: Garland Publishers, 1987.

Liston, Robert. *Slavery in America: The Heritage of Slavery.* New York: McGraw-Hill, 1972.

Shaw, Robert B. *A Legal History of Slavery in the United States.* Potsdam, NY: Northern Press, 1991.

Thirteenth Amendment

Web sites

Findlaw Internet Legal Resources. *The Thirteenth Amendment and Annotations.* [Online] http://caselaw.findlaw.com/data/constitution/amendment13/01.html (accessed July 21, 2000)

FindLaw Internet Legal Resources. *U.S. Supreme Court Opinions.* [Online] http://www.findlaw.com/casecode/supreme.html (accessed July 21, 2000).

Library of Congress's African American Odyssey Exhibit Website — Slavery — The Peculiar Institution. [Online] http://lcweb2.loc.gov (accessed September 17, 2000)

Sources

Books

Biskupic, Joan, and Elder Witt. *Guide to the U.S. Supreme Court.* 3rd ed. Washington, DC: Congressional Quarterly, 1997.

Hall, Kermit L., ed. *Oxford Companion to the Supreme Court of the United States.* New York: Oxford University Press, 1992.

Stephens, Otis H., Jr., and John M. Schebb II. *American Constitutional Law.* St. Paul, MN: West Publishing, 1993.

West's Encyclopedia of American Law. St. Paul, MN: West Group, 1999.

Fourteenth Amendment

SECTION 1. All persons born or naturalized in the United States, and subject to the jurisdiction thereof, are citizens of the United States and of the State wherein they reside. No state shall make or enforce any law that shall abridge the privileges or immunities of citizens of the United States; nor shall any State deprive any person of life, liberty, or property, without due process of law; nor deny to any person within its jurisdiction the equal protection of the laws.

SECTION 2. Representatives shall be apportioned among the several States according to their respective numbers, counting the whole number of persons in each State, excluding Indians not taxed. But when the right to vote at any election for the choice of electors for President and Vice President of the United States, Representatives in Congress, the Executive and Judicial officers of a State, or the members of the Legislature thereof, is denied to any of the male inhabitants of such State, being twenty-one years of age, and citizens of the United States, or in any way abridged, except for participation in rebellion, or other crime, the basis or representation therein shall be reduced in the proportion which the number of such male citizens shall bear to the whole number of male citizens twenty-one years of age in such State.

SECTION 3. No person shall be a Senator or Representative in Congress, or elector of President and Vice President, or hold any office, civil or military, under the United States, or under any State, who, having previously taken an oath, as a member of Congress, or as an officer of the United States, or as a member of any State legislature, or as an executive or judicial officer of any State, to support the Constitution of the United States, shall have engaged in insurrection or rebellion against the same, or given aid or comfort to the enemies thereof. But Congress may by a vote of two-thirds of each House, remove such disability.

SECTION 4. The validity of the public debt of the United States, authorized by law, including debts incurred for payment of pensions and

Fourteenth Amendment

bounties for services in suppressing insurrection or rebellion, shall not be questioned. But neither the United States nor any State shall assume or pay any debt or obligation incurred in aide of insurrection or rebellion against the United States, or any claim for the loss or emancipation of any slave; but all such debts, obligations and claims shall be held illegal and void.

SECTION 5. The Congress shall have power to enforce, by appropriate legislation, the provisions of this article.

Just as the Fifth Amendment represented a miniature Bill of Rights in itself by providing strong legal protections against federal government abuse of power, the Fourteenth Amendment extended some of these same legal safeguards against state government actions. The amendment also made blacks citizens and set penalties for aiding the South's cause during the Civil War.

The Fourteenth Amendment consists of eight basic parts, or clauses, organized in five sections, each addressing separate legal issues as follows:

- **The citizenship clause of section 1:** The original goal of this entire section was to protect the rights of the recently freed slaves. This clause identifies who may enjoy privileges of U.S. and state citizenships.

- **The privileges and immunities clause of section 1:** Declares that no state can pass laws or take action that denies an individual's rights that he or she enjoys as a U.S. citizen.

- **The due process clause of section 1:** Prohibits state governments from taking any legal actions or passing any laws that unfairly deprive a person of life, liberty, or property.

- **The equal protection clause of section 1:** Guarantees that all people should be treated fairly under state laws.

- **The apportionment clause of section 2:** Identifies how citizens of states should be represented in the U.S. House of Representatives and establishes the penalties for states if they should deny male citizens twenty-one or older the right to vote.

- **The disqualification clause of section 3:** Bans people who had previously taken an oath of office in state and federal governments

RATIFICATION FACTS

PROPOSED: Submitted by Congress to the states on June 13, 1866.

RATIFICATION: Ratified by the required three-fourths of states (twenty-eight of thirty-seven) on July 9, 1868. Declared to be part of the Constitution on July 28, 1868.

RATIFYING STATES: Connecticut, June 25, 1866; New Hampshire, July 6, 1866; Tennessee, July 19, 1866; New Jersey, September 11, 1866 (subsequently the legislature rescinded its ratification, and on March 24, 1868, readopted its resolution of rescission over the Governor's veto, and on Nov. 12, 1980, expressed support for the amendment); Oregon, September 19, 1866 (and rescinded its ratification on October 15, 1868); Vermont, October 30, 1866; Ohio, January 4, 1867 (and rescinded its ratification on January 15, 1868); New York, January 10, 1867; Kansas, January 11, 1867; Illinois, January 15, 1867; West Virginia, January 16, 1867; Michigan, January 16, 1867; Minnesota, January 16, 1867; Maine, January 19, 1867; Nevada, January 22, 1867; Indiana, January 23, 1867; Missouri, January 25, 1867; Rhode Island, February 7, 1867; Wisconsin, February 7, 1867; Pennsylvania, February 12, 1867; Massachusetts, March 20, 1867; Nebraska, June 15, 1867; Iowa, March 16, 1868; Arkansas, April 6, 1868; Florida, June 9, 1868; North Carolina, July 4, 1868 (after having rejected it on December 14, 1866); Louisiana, July 9, 1868 (after having rejected it on February 6, 1867); South Carolina, July 9, 1868 (after having rejected it on December 20, 1866).

and then actively took part in a rebellion against the United States, such as the Confederate forces, from holding any future public office in Congress or state governments, or elector of the president and vice president unless specifically exempted from the disqualification by two-thirds of each house of Congress.

- **The debt clause of section 4:** States that U.S. government debts remain valid, but debts incurred by parties supporting rebellions against the U.S. government or economic losses resulting from the freeing of slaves cannot be paid with public funds of the United States or states.

- **The enforcement clause of section 5:** States that Congress has authority to pass laws to enforce any of the parts of this amendment.

Origins of the Fourteenth Amendment

The Fourteenth Amendment was the second of three constitutional amendments adopted in the wake of the Civil War (1861–65). Collectively they became known as the Civil War amendments. Whereas the Thirteenth Amendment, ratified three years earlier in 1865, addressed the major Civil War issue of slavery, the Fourteenth addressed another key issue, states' rights.

States' rights versus a strong central government

Arguments over how much political power state governments should have were prominent from the beginning of U.S. history. After suffering from the heavy hand of the British government before gaining independence in the Revolutionary War (1775–1783), many Americans greatly distrusted strong central governments. As a result, the Articles of Confederation written in 1781 to create the first governmental system for the new nation gave almost all government powers to the states with few to the federal government. The nation was a loose union of sovereign (politically independent) states. In only a few years, the public grew to realize that the young nation's growth, particularly in business and economic matters, needed to have consistent rules and protections that only a strong central government could provide.

To correct this problem, delegates to the Constitutional Convention met in 1787. After intense debate between supporters of a much stronger central government and proponents of states' rights, a governmental structure with a stronger central government than previously existed was selected. To secure acceptance of the Constitution as it progressed through the ratification process (approval by the states), ten constitutional amendments were written to address some of the major concerns raised by states' rights supporters. The amendments, known as the Bill of Rights, were created to better guarantee protection of the states and their citizens from potentially oppressive national government powers. They were formally adopted in 1791, two years after the main body of the Constitution was ratified. The Tenth Amendment reserved all powers to the states that were not clearly given to the federal government in the Constitution or the previous nine amendments, or any amendments to be added in the future.

The controversy over the extent of states' rights, however, persisted for decades and finally boiled over as the slavery debate escalated. Seventy-seven years after the Constitution was adopted and immediately after the Civil War, whose victors supported a stronger federal government, Congress passed and the states ratified the Fourteenth Amendment. Just as the first amendments protected states and citizens from federal government actions, the Fourteenth Amendment protected citizens against state government actions. Protection for a broad range of rights including those guaranteed in the first ten amendments was extended to people denied such rights by state actions. The amendment also politically and economically penalized states and state officials who had rebelled against the U.S. government during the Civil War.

Fourteenth Amendment

The Fourteenth Amendment and the Supreme Court

Through the many years following ratification of the Fourteenth Amendment, numerous cases have involved its clauses. Some clauses have received far more courtroom attention than others. In addition, important

Some groups were taking their personal beliefs and using them as a form of law. One example is several instances of members of the Ku Klux Klan intimidating and even using violence against African Americans. Reproduced by permission of Archive Photos, Inc.

court interpretations of the clauses' intent have dramatically changed through time as U.S. society has changed.

Citizenship Clause

Controversies had long centered on how a person becomes a U.S. citizen. Often court rulings and general social tradition guided decisions on citizenship questions. As a result, through much of the nineteenth century, American citizenship was limited to certain categories of people. Excluded were such groups as black Americans and American Indians. In the infamous *Dred Scott v. Sandford* (1857) decision, Chief Justice Roger Brooke Taney (1777–1864) ruled that two categories of people held citizenship. One consisted of white people born in the United States who were descendents of U.S. citizens. The other included people born outside the United States who had entered the United States and become naturalized. Blacks, Taney said, could not become U.S. citizens, even a freeman who descended from free people. Taney added that states had the power to grant people state citizenship, but not U.S. citizenship.

Congress expands citizenship

Following the Civil War (1861–1865), Congress reversed the *Dred Scott* decision through passage of the Civil Rights Act of 1866 and then incorporated the act into the Constitution at the very beginning of section 1 of the Fourteenth Amendment. Both U.S. and state citizenship was granted to "all persons born or naturalized in the United States." The factor of where a person resides, in what jurisdiction, replaced the factor as to whether a person's ancestors or parents were citizens. Therefore, all black Americans, including the newly freed slaves, became citizens. The phrase in the amendment of "and subject to the jurisdiction thereof" eliminates those born to foreign diplomats and at that time Indians who were active members of tribes and subject to tribal law.

Based on this clause, the court ruled in *United States v. Wong Kim Ark* (1898) that a child born in the United States of Chinese parents who were not citizens did indeed become a citizen with all the rights associated with citizenship. Importantly, the court ruled in *Afroyim v. Rusk* (1967) that once a person gained U.S. citizenship, the federal government could not take citizenship away from that person against his or her will. Slowly, individual American Indians gained U.S. citizenship through various means, including the acquiring of private land beginning in the 1890s. All Indians became citizens through passage of the Indian Citizenship Act of 1924.

Privileges and Immunities Clause

During the mid-nineteenth century, supporters of a strong central government attempted to broadly interpret the privileges and immunities clause. They hoped to expand the federal government's role in regulation of business and lessen the role of the states. The Supreme Court ruled in *Slaughter House Cases* (1873) that such a broad interpretation would contradict the basic concepts of federalism in which powers are shared between the federal and state governments.

The Court ruled that Congress could not have intended such a fundamental transformation of the governmental system with this single clause especially because the amendment's primary purpose, according to the Court, was to extend U.S. citizenship to former slaves.

The actual privileges and immunities offered by the federal government to its citizens are considered very limited. These include the right of *habeas corpus* (a court order to determine the legality of a person being detained by authorities), the right to use navigable waters (water bodies deep and broad enough for boats to pass) of the United States, the right to travel freely among states, the right to petition Congress concerning grievances, the right to enter public lands, the right to vote for national public officials, the right to personal protection while in U.S. custody, the right to conduct interstate (business across state lines) commerce, and the right to acquire and retain property.

Due Process Clause

Due process is a constitutional guarantee that all legal proceedings will be fair. Before the federal or any state government may take away an individual's life, liberty, or property, the government must follow a legally set "process" that is "due" to that individual.

Legal scholars have called due process the most fundamental guarantee in American constitutional law — so important that it is promised twice in the U.S. Constitution, in the Fifth and Fourteenth amendments. Ratified in 1791 as part of the Bill of Rights, the Fifth Amendment states that no person shall "be deprived of life, liberty, or property without due process of law." Originally the Fifth applied only to actions taken by the federal government. Ratified in 1868, the Fourteenth Amendment's due process clause proclaims "[N]or shall any State deprive any person of life, liberty, or property, without due process of law." The Fourteenth's clause protected individuals from state government abuses of power.

Fourteenth Amendment

A long history

The concept of due process has a long history dating to the 1215 Magna Carta, which provided that no subject of the king of England could be imprisoned, exiled, or destroyed except by the "law of the land," — meaning only by accepted legal procedures. Sometime during the 1300s, the phrase "due process of law" was coined and had the same meaning as "law of the land." From the beginning, British colonies in America included the phrase "due process of law" in their written laws. Furthermore, even at this early date, scholars recognized that due process possessed two qualities — substantive and procedural.

In English-based legal systems, substantive due process is an expansive concept referring to the true liberties that the government may not take away from a human being. These liberties touch on every aspect of life from speech and religion to the liberty to decide whom to marry and when to have a child. By its very nature, substantive due process has required an ongoing process of defining what those true liberties are. Procedural due process, on the other hand, refers to certain rights and specific steps that must be allowed and followed for an individual to be fairly treated in legal proceedings. The scope of these legal proceedings ranges widely from situations such as criminal trials to public school placements of students in special programs.

Two paths

When the Fifth Amendment was drafted, it was unclear whether the due process clause was meant to refer to substantive qualities or procedural ones. For the first sixty years after its ratification, the narrower procedural meaning dominated in the courts and when the due process wording was used in newly written state constitutions.

Substantive due process first practically entered the U.S. jurisprudence (philosophy of law) in 1856 with the *Dred Scott* decision. Ironically, the liberty identified was the liberty for some people to own slaves — a liberty, so the court ruled, of which those people could not be deprived. In light of modern-day thinking at the beginning of the twenty-first century, this "liberty" seems outrageous, but it only serves to illustrate the evolution of liberties that at times connect to the social thinking of the time. From this point on, due process in America took two paths — a substantive one and a procedural one. The substantive path has been rocky, often at the center of heated debates, while the procedural path has been relatively smooth and remained noncontroversial.

Substantive due process and liberties

The word substantive must not be confused with the word substantial. The substantial elements of a law would consist of its goal and the rules it lays out to reach that goal. Substantive due process is concerned with the liberty behind the law. Laws could take away a liberty, protect a liberty, or even create a new liberty, all subject to the constitutionality of the action.

The ratification of the Fourteenth Amendment in 1868 allowed the courts to examine state laws that citizens claimed were depriving them of their liberties. However, through the remainder of the nineteenth century, the Supreme Court only occasionally toyed with the notion of substantive due process apart from procedural due process. The modern substantive concept emerged in 1897 with *Allgeyer v. Louisiana.*

LIBERTY OF CONTRACT. In *Allgeyer* the Court struck down a state law that prevented its citizens from contracting with out-of-state insurance companies. The Court stated that the Fourteenth Amendment guarantees all citizens the liberty to work in any legal employment and the liberty to enter into contracts relevant to that employment. Thus, the Court estab-

An unforgettable instance of the infringement of citizenship rights was the Japanese American internment camps during World War II. Reproduced by permission of the Corbis Corporation (Bellevue).

**Fourteenth
Amendment**

lished a liberty of contract. The establishment of this rather odd-sounding liberty began what has been called the freedom-of-contract version of Fourteenth Amendment substantive due process.

In the famous Supreme Court case, *Lochner v. New York* (1905), the Court struck down a New York law limiting a bakery employee's hours to ten per day and sixty per week. The owner of the bakery demanded that his bakers contract with him for many more hours than the law allowed. One of his bakers sued over the inhumane workload, saying it violated the New York Bakeshop Act. Yet, the Supreme Court ruled in the owner's favor, saying the law violated the owner's liberty to contract with his employees for however many hours he wished.

Thus, an odd twist of historical fate occurred. Rather than the Fourteenth's due process clause protecting an individual from abusive state laws, the Court used it to strike down a state law that helped individuals. Instead, the Court had chosen to protect the economic rights of business owners from any state interference. From the 1890s to 1937, the Court's primary use of the Fourteenth's substantive due process was to protect economic liberties of business owners, nearly always applying it to strike down any state law it found violated those liberties. The Court's approach reflected the economic concept of the day called *laissez faire* that allowed businesses to operate relatively free of government restraint. Protection of an individual's liberties, so important at the end of the twentieth century, had taken a backseat. In fact, the *Lochner* era was frequently criticized as a time when the Supreme Court lost its way in protecting fundamental liberties of Americans.

In the 1930s America was in the midst of the Great Depression. President Franklin D. Roosevelt (1882–1945) began his New Deal to help pull Americans out of their economic woes. Yet, the Court continued to use substantive due process business liberties to strike down drastically needed programs. With the backing of much of the U.S. population, Roosevelt threatened tactics to overcome court opposition to his programs. Roosevelt's threats were successful, and the Court changed direction. In *West Coast Hotel Co. v. Parrish* (1937) the court upheld a Washington state minimum wage law in support of its citizens' health and welfare over the business owner's liberty of contract arguments. The era during which substantive due process was almost totally associated with the business liberty to contract had come to an end.

BILL OF RIGHTS AND THE FOURTEENTH. Even before the Court abandoned its liberty of contract approach to substantive due process, it was exploring

*Equal protection
rights are extended
to everyone,
regardless of their
race, religion,
gender, or sexual
orientation.
However, under
First Amendment
rights, citizens are
free to disagree
with those rights.*

Reproduced by permission
of the Corbis Corporation
(Bellevue).

the idea of bringing the liberties spelled out in the Bill of Rights, the first
ten amendments, under the Fourteenth Amendment's due process clause.
Under the Fifth Amendment's due process clause, the liberties in the Bill
of Rights had been protected from federal government abuse, and the
Court was looking for ways to protect these substantive liberties from
state government abuse. In 1925 the court held in *Gitlow v. New York*
that the Fourteenth Amendment's due process clause could be used to
hold state governments to the free speech and press standards of the First
Amendment. *Gitlow* opened up a gradual, decades-long, case-to-case

Fourteenth Amendment

approach of incorporating the fundamental liberties listed in the Bill of Rights under Fourteenth Amendment due process protections from state government abuses. This process became known as the incorporation doctrine. At the end of the twentieth century, only the Second Amendment right to bear arms, the Third Amendment right against a person being forced to house soldiers, and the Fifth Amendment right to be indicted by a grand jury had not been brought under the Fourteenth, largely because they do not apply to states.

TWO CATEGORIES OF FUNDAMENTAL LIBERTIES. The Supreme Court has identified two categories of liberties protected by the Fourteenth Amendment's due process clause. The first are enumerated — those liberties specifically written into the Bill of Rights. Basic liberties found in the Bill of Rights include speech, religion, press, assembly, petition, and trial by jury.

The second category is the unenumerated liberties. These are liberties that are not actually written or named in the Bill of Rights but considered essential to a free society. These liberties are rooted in U.S. legal history, common law, and the moral values of the nation. No specific list of unenumerated liberties can ever be made, for they are constantly evolving with society. Supreme Court Justice Felix Frankfurter (1882–1965) explained, "Representing as it does a living principle, due process is not confined within a permanent catalogue of what may at a given time be deemed the limits or the essentials of fundamental rights."

THE NEW SUBSTANTIVE DUE PROCESS. In the 1850s, liberty to own slaves was an unenumerated right protected by substantive due process. In the 1890s to 1930s, the unenumerated right that received the most attention and protection under substantive due process was the liberty of contract. Beginning in the 1960s, the court used substantive due process to protect the civil liberties of individuals, especially racial minorities and women, against state government actions. Sometimes called the "new" substantive due process, unenumerated liberties in matters of personal choice in family life began to dominate. The liberty to make choices in the most personal dilemmas of life and death is referred to as the general right to privacy.

THE LIBERTY OF PRIVACY. The liberty of privacy, or the right to privacy, recognizes under substantive due process the right of individuals to lead their private lives free from unreasonable government interference. Examples of privacy issues on which the court has ruled include birth control, abortion, extended family living arrangements, and the right to die.

Under a 1879 Connecticut law, Estelle Griswold was convicted of the crime of counseling married couples on the use of birth control and contraceptives. The defendant argued there existed a constitutional right to privacy, although not specifically written in the Constitution, which prevents the government from intruding into certain areas of a person's life. Writing for the majority, Justice William O. Douglas (1898–1980) pulled together parts of the First, Fourth, Fifth, and Ninth amendments that indeed implied "zones of privacy that are the foundation for a general right to privacy." He wrote in *Griswold v. Connecticut* (1965) that substantive due process of the Fourteenth Amendment may be used to limit state government interference with the right to privacy.

Eisenstadt v. Baird (1972) and *Carey v. Population Services International* (1977) made it clear that the *Griswold* decision could be extended to privacy interests of unmarried people and minors, who could not be denied access to contraceptives.

In 1973 Jane Roe argued that Texas abortion laws were unconstitutional and violated her rights under substantive due process of the Fourteenth Amendment. In *Roe v. Wade* the Court ruled in Roe's favor, finding that both the Fourteenth Amendment and the Ninth Amendment encompassed an unenumerated liberty for a woman to decide whether to terminate her pregnancy.

In 1977, *Moore v. City of East Cleveland* the Court struck down local ordinances that limited the number of occupants that could live in particular dwellings, which shut out extended family members such as grandparents.

The liberty of privacy issues moved into the 1990s asking whether the right to die is a protected liberty. In *Cruzan v. Director of Missouri Department of Health* (1990) Chief Justice William Rehnquist (1924–) supported "the right of a competent individual to refuse medical treatment" (right to die). He wrote that the right to die is a "constitutionally protected liberty interest" under the Fourteenth Amendment due process of law. At the end of the 1990s, the court ruled on "physician-assisted suicide" in *Washington et al. v. Glucksberg et al.* (1997). The Court refused to recognize physician-assisted suicide as an "unenumerated" liberty; therefore, there was no Fourteenth Amendment substantive due process to strike down a Washington law banning "assisted suicide." The Washington law stood.

The right of privacy does not protect all forms of behavior behind closed doors. There is no constitutional protection for situations such as

Fourteenth Amendment

While the Fourteenth Amendment does not allow anyone to be discriminated against because of their religion, it still does not allow for the practice of religion in public institutions, such as public schools. Reproduced by permission of The Picture Cube.

viewing child pornography or soliciting prostitutes. The liberty interest will allow government intervention as long as there is a rational purpose behind the intervention.

Procedural due process

While substantive due process looks at the liberty behind the law, procedural due process considers only the manner in which government acts. Procedural due process limits the exercise of power of state and federal governments by requiring they follow certain steps or procedures that will allow all forms of legal proceedings to be fair. Justice Frankfurter described the promise of fundamental fairness as "representing a profound attitude of fairness between man and man, and more particularly between the individual and the government." Before a government can deprive an individual of life, liberty, or property, it must follow due process of law or standard accepted legal procedures.

The Bill of Rights contains legal practices that are key to procedural due process. Through the second half of the twentieth century, most of the first ten amendments making up the Bill of Rights were brought

under the umbrella of the Fourteenth Amendment's due process and applied to the legal proceedings of states. Previously, the standards in those amendments had applied only to federal proceedings under the Fifth Amendment's due process. For example, in *Gideon v. Wainwright* (1963) the Court ruled that the right to counsel (to have an attorney) was so fundamental that the Fourteenth Amendment's due process clause extended to the Sixth Amendment guarantee of counsel to every defendant in a state criminal trial, just as in a federal trial.

Likewise, in *Malloy v. Hogan* (1964), the Court extended the protection to not be forced to incriminate oneself found in the Fifth Amendment to state proceedings under the Fourteenth's due process. No longer could states force confessions. Individuals in state trials could now "take the Fifth," that is have the right to remain silent when accused and to refuse to testify in one's own defense.

The many standard legal procedures in criminal cases include: the right to be told of the crime being charged; protection from unreasonable searches and seizures; double jeopardy, or to not be tried more than once for the same crime; a speedy, public trial by an impartial jury; right to cross-examination; and, that the state prove charges beyond a reasonable doubt.

In addition to criminal trials, procedural due process extends protections in many facets of government-individual interactions, such as government entitlement programs including Social Security and welfare, licensing procedures, and public school placements. Generally individuals must be given notice of a proceeding concerning them and be given an opportunity to speak in their behalf before the government acts to take a right away from them. For example, *Bell v. Burson* (1971) established that a license to drive a car is a constitutional right and cannot be revoked without a hearing. In public schools, the parents of a child receiving special education services may request a due process hearing if they disagree with the identification, evaluation, placement, or other aspect related to their child's public education.

What is a person?

The meaning of "person" in the due process clause, and in the equal protection clause, has received Court attention. In *Yick Wo v. Hopkins* (1886) the Court held that the due process clause protects all humans regardless of race, color, or citizenship. Then in *Grosjean v. American Press Co.* (1936) the Court held that although corporations are not consid-

JOSEPH LOCHNER, AMAN SCHMITTER, AND THE LIBERTY OF CONTRACT

Joseph Lochner, a small bakery owner in Utica, New York, produced biscuits, breads, and cakes for early-morning customers. His employees frequently had to work late at the night, often sleeping in the bakery and rising in time to have the goods ready for customers. In April 1901, one of Lochner's bakers, Aman Schmitter, worked more than sixty hours in one week, violating the recently passed Bakeshop Act of 1895, which set sanitation standards and maximum work hours. A complaint was filed with the police, who arrested Lochner and charged him in violation of the Bakeshop Act.

Found guilty and sentenced to pay a fifty-dollar fine or spend fifty days in jail, Lochner appealed his case arguing that New York's Bakeshop Act interfered with his constitutional freedom to make a contract with his employees concerning pay and hours of work. This interfered with his right to earn a living and pursue a lawful trade as provided in the Fourteenth Amendment's due process clause.

ered persons in the context of "liberty" protected by the amendment, corporations may still not be deprived of their property without due process of law. They deserve protection from oppressive state laws just as individuals.

Equal Protection Clause

An American belief in fairness is basic to present-day U.S. society. Consequently, the use of personal traits such as race, gender (sex of the person), or nationality to legally set apart one group of people from others quickly raises serious concerns over constitutional appropriateness. However, this modern notion of equality is not the same as it was when America was very young. Although the 1776 Declaration of Independence proclaimed that "all Men are created equal" with certain basic rights including "Life, Liberty, and the Pursuit of Happiness," the goal of gaining national liberty from England was stronger than striving for individual equality among the colonists. As a result, some classes of people enjoyed more rights than others. For example, in the first years of the

Losing in the New York court system, Lochner took his case to the U.S. Supreme Court where he argued the law violated his "liberty of contract." He argued that because baking was not a dangerous occupation, the state law was an inappropriate use of police powers that deprived bakery owners due process rights. New York argued such state protections for the health and well-being of workers and general public were nothing new. Such laws were needed for the public good to protect workers from being unfairly exploited.

The Court's resulting decision reflected the general sentiments of a growing young industrial society that believed that the least amount of government regulation would allow the economy to grow "naturally." The Court created an unwritten right in *Lochner* from a loose reading of the Fourteenth Amendment's due process clause regarding liberty and the right to contract. Such an interpretation persisted for decades with an emphasis on property rights and liberty of contract. This perspective was later replaced in the last half of the twentieth century with an emphasis on protecting individual civil rights from police power. State governments then were given considerable freedom to regulate the workplace and other economic affairs.

nation, only white male adult citizens who owned property could vote. Excluded were women, people of color, and the poor who held no property. In addition, slavery played an important role in the nation's economy. In fact, nowhere did the term equality appear in the U.S. Constitution adopted in 1789 or the Bill of Rights of 1791.

Even following adoption of the Fourteenth Amendment's equal protection clause, many white Americans did not think in terms of social equality in the late nineteenth and early twentieth centuries. Racial prejudice was rampant. The U.S. Supreme Court was not a source of support for black Americans. It consistently issued decisions greatly limiting what the government could do to protect the rights of blacks and enforce the Fourteenth Amendment.

Equal treatment of America's diverse population, therefore, did not immediately follow from the amendment. When cases involving equality issues were first brought before federal courts, including the U.S. Supreme Court, the courts consistently interpreted the Fourteenth Amendment narrowly (very limited in meaning). The first key interpretation

Fourteenth Amendment

Rosa Parks being fingerprinted after being arrested for refusing to give up her seat to a white man on a Montgomery bus.

Reproduced by permission of AP/Wide World Photos.

came in 1883 in the *Civil Rights Cases* involving the Civil Rights Act of 1875 passed by Congress to enforce the Civil War amendments. This act sought to assure equal access to public transportation and public places such as inns and theaters. The Supreme Court ruled that the Fourteenth Amendment only applied to discrimination by state governments, not to discrimination by private people such as owners of railroads, theaters, or inns. The ruling largely overturned (negated) the 1875 act, leaving the federal government virtually powerless to control discrimination against blacks by private individuals. Taking advantage of this powerlessness, the governments of many Southern states created segregation (separation of groups by race) laws in the 1880s known as Jim Crow laws.

Separate but equal

The next major setback in enforcement of the equal protection clause was the *Plessy v. Ferguson* (1896) decision. In reaction to those seeking true equality in access to public facilities (places), the Court established the "separate but equal" rule. The rule meant that violation of the clause would not occur as long as black Americans had access to the same kind of facilities as whites, even if they were separate from those

used by whites. This ruling led to black Americans and whites having separate water fountains, separate public restrooms, and separate schools. The ruling basically promoted racial segregation by offering a very narrow interpretation of equal protection.

The ruling would greatly influence social customs in the United States, particularly in the South, for most of the next six decades. Rarely would separate black facilities be as good as white facilities, and given the lengthy history of discrimination in America, blacks held little political power to make sure separate facilities would become equal in quality. The phrase "separate but equal" became symbolic of forced racial segregation in the nation invading almost every aspect of American society, including restaurants, railroads, streetcars, waiting rooms, parks, cemeteries, churches, hospitals, prisons, elevators, theaters, schools, public rest rooms, water fountains, and even public telephones.

Aliens and equal protection

Ironically, aliens (citizens from foreign countries) initially received more favorable treatment from the courts concerning equal protection than

Fourteenth Amendment

When the schools were desegregated in the South, the National Guard had to be called in to escort African American students to school in Little Rock, Arkansas.

Reproduced by permission of AP/Wide World Photos.

black Americans. In *Yick Wo v. Hopkins* (1886) the Supreme Court ruled in favor of a Chinese laundry owner. The owner claimed a San Francisco city ordinance (law) regulating business licenses, although containing no discriminatory wording, was written in such a way to shut down Chinese laundry businesses in the city. *Yick Wo* was the only successful equal protection challenge among the first cases brought to the Supreme Court in the decades following the ratification of the Fourteenth Amendment.

The shift to individual civil rights

The historically important shift in applying the equal protection clause to individual civil rights began to occur in the late 1930s through efforts of the National Association for the Advancement of Colored Peoples (NAACP) and other groups. The courts responded with favorable decisions for racial minorities suffering injustices under state law. For example, in *Missouri ex rel. Gaines v. Canada* (1938) the Supreme Court ruled in favor of an individual denied entrance into a state law school. The Court found that a state requirement based solely on race violated the equal protection clause.

The modern civil rights era

Two major 1954 court decisions introduced the modern civil rights era and brought the equal protection clause to the forefront of constitutional law in the mid-twentieth century. In the landmark case of *Brown v. Board of Education,* the Supreme Court struck down *Plessy*'s "separate but equal" rule by finding that public school segregation was unconstitutional (not following the intent of the U.S. Constitution). A civil rights revolution was begun. That same year in *Bolling v. Sharpe* the Court held that the due process clause in the Fifth Amendment prohibited racial discrimination by the federal government just as the equal protection clause of the Fourteenth Amendment prohibits discrimination by state governments. The decision essentially extended the equal protection clause of the Fourteenth Amendment to the due process clause of the Fifth Amendment. The door was opened to a dramatically broader protection of individuals' civil rights.

Still, progress in recognizing individual civil rights in the United States following decades of racial discrimination was slow. Numerous public protests followed, often involving highly publicized acts of civil disobedience (peacefully disobeying laws considered unjust) under the leadership of Dr. Martin Luther King, Jr. (1929–1968) and others. Eventually in the mid-1960s, widespread violence erupted in the nation's cities.

Congress reacted to the growing social unrest by passing a series of laws designed to further recognize civil rights and equality under the law for minorities and women. The 1963 Equal Pay Act required that men and women receive similar pay for performing similar work. The landmark 1964 Civil Rights Act prohibited discrimination based on race, color, national origin, or religion at most privately owned businesses that serve the public. The 1964 act also established equal opportunity in employment on the basis of race, religion, and sex. In *Reynolds v. Sims* (1964) the Court extended equal protection under the Fourteenth Amendment to voters' rights. The "one person, one vote" rule resulting from the decision was put into law by Congress the following year in the 1965 Voting Rights Act. Prohibited were state residency requirements, poll taxes (pay a tax before voting), and candidate filing fees that traditionally were used to discriminate against poorer minority voters. A fourth important law followed in 1968 with the Fair Housing Act, which prohibited discrimination in housing.

Fourteenth Amendment

Expanding protections

Court decisions involving the equal protection clause began focusing more on gender discrimination as the public began demanding equal treatment of the sexes. In 1971, the Court in *Reed v. Reed* overturned a state law arbitrarily discriminating against women, thus extending the equal protection clause to gender discrimination. Courts also found some laws discriminatory against illegitimate children (whose parents were not married), and unwed fathers. In *Weber v. Aetna Casualty & Surety Co.* (1972) the court ruled that illegitimate children should have the same protections as other children. They should not be penalized through life for their parents' actions over which they had no control. Through the 1980s and 1990s, equal protection issues tackled new topics such as sexual harassment, gay rights, affirmative action (vigorous encouragement of increased representation of women and minorities), and assisted suicide (right to choose when to die).

Standards of scrutiny

Despite the considerably broadened application, the equal protection clause does not require that all people be treated equally at all times. Discrimination is sometimes legally permitted, such as not allowing people younger than eighteen to vote in elections. The key decision often before the courts is to determine when discrimination is justified. With this in mind, the Court created a system of three different levels of exam-

REACTION TO OLIVER BROWN'S COURT VICTORY

The landmark 1954 Supreme Court decision in *Brown v. Board of Education, Topeka, Kansas,* represented a major turning point in constitutional law and legal history concerning recognition of individual civil rights. But it was the public reaction to the decision that actually inspired additional aggressive steps by the federal government toward ending racial discrimination. The case addressed one of the most basic, and emotional, issues in America: the education of its children.

Not surprisingly the case involved seemingly simple issues. Oliver Brown, a black man and railroad welder living in Topeka, Kansas, wanted to send one of his daughters, Linda, a third-grader, to the closest public school, rather than one designated for blacks that was not only farther away, but was a mile on the other side of a dangerous railroad switching yard.

But, like many states in the mid-twentieth century, public schools were racially segregated under Kansas state law. Topeka had twenty-two public elementary schools with four set aside for black schoolchildren. When Topeka school officials refused to let his daughter enroll in the nearby white school, Brown filed charges claiming that racial segregation of public schools denied black schoolchildren equal protection of the law as guaranteed by the Fourteenth Amendment. Local courts ruled against Brown, holding that school segregation does not violate the Constitution according to the separate but equal doctrine described in the earlier Supreme Court decision of *Plessy v. Ferguson* (1896). Brown appealed the decision to the U.S. Supreme Court. The Court ruled unanimously in Brown's favor agreeing that racial segregation is always unequal regardless of whether the black children had the same quality of facilities, teachers, and books. Chief Justice Earl Warren (1891–1974)

ination, called scrutiny, to test an action or law for equal protection violations. A case receives the highest level of scrutiny or "strict scrutiny" if it involves racial discrimination, aliens, or issues of nationality. At the intermediate level of scrutiny are cases involving women and "illegitimate persons" (individuals whose parents were not married). All other cases involving equal protection considerations fall into what is called

wrote, "Today, education is perhaps the most important function of the state and local governments ... It is required in the performance of our most basic public responsibilities ... It is the very foundation of good citizenship. Today it is a principal instrument in awakening the child to cultural values, in preparing him for later professional training, and in helping him to adjust normally to his environment ... Such an opportunity ... is a right which must be made available to all on equal terms."

By reversing the *Plessy* ruling and throwing out the "separate but equal" doctrine, the Court touched off strong political and public opposition. More than a hundred members of Congress from the South signed a statement urging states to resist enforcement of the decision. Even President Dwight D. Eisenhower (1890–1969) refused to support the decision. New schemes were adopted to keep schools segregated, public funding of private segregated schools was attempted, and some districts even closed public schools. In 1957 the U.S. Army and the Arkansas National Guard were called to protect black children being admitted to a Little Rock high school. In 1962 President John F. Kennedy (1917–1963) sent federal troops to the University of Mississippi when James Meredith attempted to enroll.

Ten years after the *Brown* decision, fewer than two percent of black schoolchildren in the South were attending schools with whites. With the violence and resistance persisting, public pressure mounted for a resolution. Congress passed the Civil Rights Act of 1964. The act established sweeping prohibitions against racial discrimination in public places, including schools, and gave the U.S. attorney general authority to initiate court actions against school districts resisting the *Brown* decision. By the early 1970s, school segregation policies had been largely eliminated. Meanwhile, the ruling had also set the stage for ending racial segregation in other public places, from bus stations to public libraries to restrooms.

"rational basis" scrutiny. It is generally far easier to justify a law as rational rather than defending it under strict scrutiny.

Changing government roles under equal protection

The role of government regarding protection of citizens' civil rights has changed dramatically since the late nineteenth century. Originally the government was mainly concerned with protecting a person's activities from government restriction unless the person's behavior was extreme or posed a danger to others. In a fundamental shift in philosophy, the government had shifted emphasis to promoting community general welfare by the late twentieth century. This philosophical shift was reflected in society as a whole. Limiting the behavior or actions of some people in order to protect the rights of others had become acceptable. For example, restaurant owners are required to serve all members of the public, whether they want to or not, unless questions of safety or health arise. This change, in which the Fourteenth Amendment played a key role, represented a shift in emphasis from political liberty from government rules during the eighteenth century colonial period to ensuring equality for all in the later years of the twentieth century. The equal protection clause has become the primary constitutional shield for protecting the civil rights of the many groups of people in the United States.

Apportionment Clause

Although some supported granting newly freed slaves voting rights following the Civil War, general public sentiment remained largely opposed. Blacks could vote in only a few Northern states. In addition, according to Article I of the Constitution, black slaves only counted as three-fifths of person when determining how much representation a state could have in the U.S. House of Representation. The abolition of slavery by the Thirteenth Amendment in 1865 meant that black Americans became fully counted. Each state's representation was based on its total population. This sudden potential increase in representation for Southern states substantially changed the apportionment of seats in the U.S. House of Representatives and meant the newly readmitted states would have even greater political clout than before. To assure the representatives would be white, Southerners as well as Democrats in the North adamantly opposed a constitutional amendment granting voting rights for blacks.

There was substantial political opposition to granting the black vote within the Fourteenth Amendment, so section 2 of the amendment containing the apportionment clause was written as a compromise. This clause replaced the three-fifths rule in Article I. Any state denying male citizens twenty-one years of age or older the right to vote would have its representation in Congress decreased accordingly. The amendment did allow states to deny the vote to criminals.

The section, however, never became a political factor because the Fifteenth Amendment granting voting rights to black Americans was ratified two years later. In 1972, the Supreme Court did use the apportionment clause in *Richardson v. Ramirez* to rule that a convicted felon had no right to vote, even after completing a prison sentence. The Court stated that the apportionment clause overrode the equal protection clause in such situations.

Disqualification Clause

Section 3 of the amendment disqualified people who aided the South in the Civil War from holding public office. People affected were those who had previously held public office in the federal or state governments and had taken oaths to uphold the U.S. Constitution. This clause attempted to keep Confederate leaders out of power. Congress, by a vote of two-thirds of each House, could reinstate individuals affected. This occurred on several occasions. In 1872 Congress passed a law limiting the disqualification to individuals in certain offices, and the ban was removed altogether in 1898.

Public Debt Clause

Section 4 of the amendment guaranteed the repayment of debts the U.S. government incurred during the Civil War, such as payment of pensions to soldiers. Congress sought to assure the public and its debtors that the government's debts would be paid and not eliminated by any congressional acts or court decisions. As late as 1935, the Court used the section to limit congressional powers in altering debt payments in *Perry v. United States.* The public debt clause also stated that debts incurred by the Confederacy in rebellion against the United States were not part of these public debts. This clause prevented Southern states from using money to pay for the rebellion or to pay citizens who lost their slaves.

Enforcement Clause

Section 5 of the amendment granted Congress power to pass laws enforcing the Fourteenth Amendment's various clauses. Congress, shortly after ratification, passed seven laws to enact the amendment including several general civil rights acts banning racial discrimination. The Court consistently refused to acknowledge that the enforcement clause enlarged Con-

**Fourteenth
Amendment**

gress's power to protect individual rights. By the end of the century, most of the laws had been overturned by the court, directly repealed, or made obsolete by later legislation. Not until the civil rights revolution of the 1950s and 1960s did the Civil War amendments take on the meaning the authors intended.

Summing the Parts of the Fourteenth Amendment

The main goal of the Fourteenth Amendment, ratified (approved) in 1868, was to extend citizenship to the newly freed slaves and to guarantee their civil rights as interpreted by Congress. Civil rights referred to the idea of all citizens being able to participate free from discrimination (giving privileges to one group but not another) in such public activities as voting, staying in an inn, attending a theater performance, or seeking employment.

Some clauses in the amendment, including the apportionment, disqualification, and debt clauses, addressed immediate concerns created by the South's rebellion against the Union leading to the Civil War. Other clauses were more long lasting, affecting everyday life in U.S. society. Two of the key clauses in the Fourteenth Amendment are the due process and equal protection clauses. Due process extends to citizens protections from potentially unfair state government laws and actions similar to the Fifth Amendment that protects citizens and states from unfair federal government actions. The idea of equality under the law was expressed for the first time in the Constitution in the Fourteenth Amendment's equal protection clause. Equal protection of the laws means no person will be denied the same protection of the laws enjoyed by other people or groups. The Fourteenth's due process and equal protection clauses have played a significant role in recognizing individual civil rights in numerous court decisions through the second half of the twentieth century.

For More Information

Books

Cashman, Sean D. *African Americans and the Quest for Civil Rights, 1900–1990.* New York: New York University Press, 1991.

Howard, John R. *The Shifting Wind: The Supreme Court and Civil Rights From Reconstruction to Brown.* Albany: State University of New York Press, 1999.

Levine, Michael L. *African Americans and Civil Rights: From 1619 to the Present.* Phoenix, AZ: Oryx Press, 1996.

Medearis, Angela S. *Come This Far to Freedom: A History of African Americans.* New York: Athenum, 1993.

Myers, Walter D. *Now Is Your Time! The African-American Struggle for Freedom.* New York: HarperTrophy, 1991.

Thermstrom, Stephan, and Abigail Thermstrom. *America in Black and White: One Nation, Indivisible.* New York: Simon & Schuster, 1999.

Web sites

Findlaw Internet Legal Resources. *The Fourteenth Amendment and Annotations.* [Online] http://caselaw.findlaw.com/data/constitution/amendment14/01.html (accessed July 21, 2000)

FindLaw Internet Legal Resources. *U.S. Supreme Court Opinions.* [Online] http://www.findlaw.com/casecode/supreme.html (accessed July 21, 2000).

National Association for the Advancement of Colored People (NAACP) . [Online] http://www.naacp.org (accessed August 30, 2000)

Fourteenth Amendment

Sources

Books

Biskupic, Joan, and Elder Witt. *Guide to the U.S. Supreme Court.* Third ed. Washington, DC: Congressional Quarterly, 1997.

Hall, Kermit L., ed. *Oxford Companion to the Supreme Court of the United States.* New York: Oxford University Press, 1992.

Stephens, Otis H., Jr., and John M. Schebb II. *American Constitutional Law.* St. Paul, MN: West Publishing, 1993.

West's Encyclopedia of American Law. St. Paul, MN: West Group, 1997.

Fifteenth Amendment

SECTION 1. The right of citizens of the United States to vote shall not be denied or abridged by the United States or by any State on account of race, color, or previous condition of servitude.

SECTION 2. The Congress shall have power to enforce this article by appropriate legislation.

In most democracies, including the United States, the right to vote means a citizen's right to periodically choose in free elections among candidates who offer different views. Although the freedom to vote is considered a foundation of democracy, nowhere did the original U.S. Constitution name voting as a right of U.S. citizens. Rather the right was implied (not directly expressed but suggested) in several sections of the Constitution. For example, the Constitution guarantees that every state will have a republican form of government (government officials are elected by voters) and it states that the U.S. House of Representatives is "chosen ... by the People of the several States." It also refers to the election of senators and the president. The matter of who would have the right to vote was left entirely to individual states, which determined their own sets of voter qualifications, even for national elections. The Fifteenth Amendment was passed to directly address voting rights of the freed slaves. The amendment's brief text focused on the single issue of equal treatment to all races. The matter of establishing voter qualifications was still left strictly to the states; hence, in reality, the amendment's intensions were long ignored.

Origins of the Fifteenth Amendment

After the Revolutionary War (1775-1783), only males with property could vote in America. This practice of equating ownership of property

Fifteenth
Amendment

RATIFICATION FACTS

PROPOSED: Submitted by Congress to the states on February 26, 1869.

RATIFICATION: Ratified by the required three-fourths of states (twenty-eight of thirty-seven) on February 17, 1870. Declared to be part of the Constitution on March 30, 1870.

RATIFYING STATES: Nevada, March 1, 1869; West Virginia, March 3, 1869; Illinois, March 5, 1869; Louisiana, March 5, 1869; North Carolina, March 5, 1869; Michigan, March 8, 1869; Wisconsin, March 9, 1869; Maine, March 11, 1869; Massachusetts, March 12, 1869; Arkansas, March 15, 1869; South Carolina, March 15, 1869; Pennsylvania, March 25, 1869; New York, April 14, 1869 (and the legislature of the same State passed a resolution January 5, 1870, to withdraw its consent to it, which action it rescinded on March 30, 1870); Indiana, May 14, 1869; Connecticut, May 19, 1869; Florida, June 14, 1869; New Hampshire, July 1, 1869; Virginia, October 8, 1869; Vermont, October 20, 1869; Missouri, January 7, 1870; Minnesota, January 13, 1870; Mississippi, January 17, 1870; Rhode Island, January 18, 1870; Kansas, January 19, 1870; Ohio, January 27, 1870 (after having rejected it on April 30, 1869); Georgia, February 2, 1870; Iowa, February 3, 1870.

with the right to vote followed a long English tradition dating to the fifteenth century. Because land was readily available in the new nation, many men held land and could therefore vote. Leaders of the new nation, among them the framers of the Constitution, feared that giving too much power to the citizens could result in mob rule. Therefore, they believed some restrictions should be imposed on the right to vote. The prevailing belief was that owning property would give men a greater stake in society and, consequently, make them more responsible to act in the public interest at the voting booth. Early citizens considered voting a privilege, not a right.

In keeping with the concept of federalism that called for splitting governmental powers between the state and national governments, the framers in 1787 largely left it to the states to determine who could vote. The states uniformly applied the property owning standard. Hence the right

to vote was limited to those individuals owning property, and even those voting citizens could only directly elect their state legislators and representatives to the U.S. House of Representatives. To check the power of the people, state legislators elected the president and U.S. senators.

Some free blacks in northern states had property and could vote in the first decades of the nation's history. The rise of Jacksonian democracy in the 1830s, which emphasized populist beliefs (the common citizens should hold greater political power), led to demands for greater voting rights and giving common people a greater say in government. Ironically, as voting requirements eased in response

President Andrew Jackson held the popular belief that the citizens should hold the greatest political power. Courtesy of the Library of Congress.

to the growing unpopularity of the property requirements, blacks were not able to benefit from the laxer requirements. Several factors were responsible. In general, many whites distrusted blacks and claimed they lacked civic virtue. In addition, during this time Democratic Party politicians held considerable power and opposed ending slavery. Therefore, they did not want to give blacks the opportunity to support antislavery candidates at the ballot box.

By the beginning of the Civil War in 1861, most states prohibited the black vote outright or enforced property or education qualifications that ruled out most free blacks. Even while antislavery sentiments grew and the free black population increased, support for black suffrage (right to vote in public elections) did not significantly grow. Thus, states were free to restrict the black vote however they saw fit. As an example, New York adopted a new constitution in 1846 dropping property qualifications for whites but not blacks.

Following the Civil War (1861–1865), many whites, particularly in the South, wanted to keep the freed blacks as close to servitude as possible despite adoption in 1865 of the Thirteenth Amendment banning slavery. Only in Tennessee, where Republicans controlled the government, did blacks have the right to vote in the South. The Democrats blocked the black vote elsewhere in the Southern region. Blacks could vote in New England states, except for Connecticut, and in several midwestern states. In early 1867, Congress passed the First Military Reconstruction Act, which made the granting of voting rights to black males a requirement for readmission to the Union in ten Southern states. Limited in its extent, the act did not apply to states outside the South where blacks did not have the vote.

By the end of 1867, under the federal army rule of Reconstruction, about seven hundred thousand Southern black men were registered to vote. These newly registered voters helped select delegates to form new state governments and elect officials to run the new governments.

Fifteenth Amendment

An 1866 racist poster attacking the postwar efforts of the Republicans to pass a constitutional amendment granting blacks more rights.

Courtesy of the Library of Congress.

GEARY
Is for Negro Suffrage.

STEVENS
Advocates it.

FORNEY
Howls for it.

McCLURE
Speaks for it.

CAMERON
Wants it.

TheLEAGUE
Sustains it.

They are rich, and want to make

The Negro the Equal
OF THE POOR WHITE MAN,
and then rule them both

POLLS

The BLACK Roll
CANDIDATES FOR CONGRESS
WHO VOTED FOR THIS BILL.

THAD. STEVENS
WM. D. KELLEY
CHAS. O'NEILL
LEONARD MYERS
JNO. M. BROOMALL
GEORGE F. MILLER
STEPHEN F. WILSON
ULYSSES MERCUR
GEO. V. LAWRENCE
GLENNI W. SCHOFIELD
J. K. MOORHEAD
THOMAS WILLIAMS

THE RADICAL PLATFORM--"NEGRO SUFFRAGE THE ONLY ISSUE!"
Every man who votes for Geary or for a Radical Candidate for Congress, votes as surely for Negro Suffrage and Negro Equality, as if they were printed on his ballot.

Fifteenth Amendment

In 1868 the Fourteenth Amendment, the second of the three Civil War amendments, was adopted. It extended to citizens a broad range of constitutional protections from state government actions. However, the amendment avoided reference to voting rights because little support existed nationally to grant black Americans the right to vote. The responsibility to determine voter qualifications remained with the states.

Passage of the Fifteenth Amendment

The black vote helped elect Republican candidate Ulysses S. Grant (1822–1885) as president in 1868. Though Grant won handily, Democrats were able to gain seats in Congress. Given the persistent efforts of white Southern Democrats to discourage black Republican votes through intimidation, the Republicans decided something had to be done before the newly elected Democrats could take the seats they had won and take control of Congress. In early 1869, a new constitutional amendment was proposed stimulated by the idea of equal access to the voting booth.

At the time Congress was divided largely into three political factions: (1) those opposing any other amendment addressing minority rights after the recent passage of the Thirteenth and Fourteenth amendments; (2) those wanting suffrage for all males with no voting requirements; and, (3) those in the middle wishing to ban racial discrimination in voting but still leave determination of voting requirements to the states. The latter group prevailed.

Anticipating a difficult political battle, compromises were made to increase public acceptance of the amendment. A proposed guarantee that some blacks would hold office was dropped in the final draft as well as a ban on state literacy, property, and nativity (place of birth) tests.

Not surprisingly, the fight for ratification (state approval) followed party lines. The Republicans supported the amendment; the Democrats opposed it. However, ratification of the amendment by Southern states was assured because it was required for readmission to the Union. The fight was most dramatic in the border states of the lower North, which had a mixture in their state legislatures of Republicans and Democrats. Nevertheless, after intense debates, the amendment was formally ratified on March 30, 1870, guaranteeing citizens the privilege of voting free of any restrictions based upon race, color, or previous servitude.

With ratification of the Fifteenth Amendment, black males were given the vote in seventeen more Northern and border states. It also reaffirmed voting rights in those states that recognized the black vote.

Republicans vigorously touted the Fifteenth Amendment as the ultimate achievement of Reconstruction.

The Fifteenth Amendment and the Supreme Court

The rights and protections expressed in the Fifteenth Amendment appear rather brief and straightforward. Section 1 of the Fifteenth Amendment prohibits state or federal governments from denying U.S. citizens the right to vote "on account of race, color, or previous condition of servitude." Section 2 grants Congress powers to pass laws enforcing section 1. However, as was the case with the three Civil War amendments in general, progress in enforcing the new rights came very slowly.

Section 1: Prohibiting Racial Discrimination in Voting

Section 1's promotion of the black vote was met with strong resistance throughout the South. Intimidation became increasingly violent by such white supremacist organizations as the Ku Klux Klan, which aimed to prevent blacks from voting. The Klan's hooded midnight riders terrorized blacks by burning crops, and whipping, clubbing, and murdering victims. Congress passed laws in the 1870s banning terrorist activities and establishing stiff penalties for interfering with black voters, but they proved difficult to enforce in many areas sympathetic to the white terrorists.

As Reconstruction was drawing to an end in 1877, efforts to enforce social and economic change dwindled. It soon became evident that section 1 of the Fifteenth Amendment on its own was ineffective. Blacks' voting rights began steadily eroding even in the northern border states.

By 1900, all eleven former Confederate states made it virtually impossible for blacks to vote. The southern states carefully worded their voting requirements to avoid obvious Fifteenth Amendment section 1 violations. As long as state voter eligibility requirements did not openly discriminate on the basis of "race, color, or previous condition of servitude" they were not considered in violation of the amendment. Though appearing to apply to all men equally, in actuality the requirements were directed against people of color. States used a variety of measures to exclude the black vote: literacy tests, white-only primaries, poll taxes, and grandfather clauses. These techniques proved successful in excluding blacks from political participation until the mid-1960s. Consequently, whites completely dominated all levels of government in the southern states for at least a century following the Civil War.

Fifteenth Amendment

Literacy tests were one way in which local governments tried to keep blacks from voting.

Grandfather clauses and literacy tests

By the 1890s, grandfather clauses and literacy tests were a popular combination of voter eligibility requirements in the South. Grandfather clauses required all voters to show that their ancestors were eligible to vote in 1866. Blacks in 1890 had no ancestors who were eligible to vote in 1866. If people could not show proof of 1866 voting ancestors, they had to pass a literacy (ability to read) test. First adopted by Mississippi in 1890, this strategy rapidly spread throughout the South. Nearly all black men were disqualified from voting. As was often the case, most whites did not have to take literacy tests, even though many could not read, because typically most white men had ancestors eligible to vote in 1866. Black voter registration in Mississippi dropped from approximately 70 percent of black adult males in 1890 to under 6 percent by 1892. When challenged in courts, states contended the Fifteenth Amendment was not violated because all voter applicants had to either meet the requirements of the grandfather clause or pass a literacy test. The Supreme Court was of no help, ruling that literacy tests as well as poll taxes (fees charged at the voting place) were legal in *Williams v. Mississippi* (1898).

EXCERPTS FROM THE CONSTITUTION

Part 1. In case of the removal of the president from office, or of his death, resignation, or inability to discharge the powers and duties of the said office, the same shall devolve on the vice-president, and the congress may by law provide for the case of removal, death, resignaton or inability, both of the president and vice-president, declaring what officer shall then act as president, and such officer shall act accordingly, until the disability be removed, or a president shall be elected.

Part 2. In all cases affecting ambassadors, other public ministers and consuls, and those in which a state shall be a party, the supreme court shall have original jurisdiction.

Part 3. In all the other cases before mentioned, the supreme court shall have appellate jurisdiction, both as to law and fact, with such exceptions, and under such regulations as the congress shall make.

Part 4. Neither slavery nor involuntary servitude, except as a punishment for crime whereof the party shall have been duly convicted, shall exist within the United States, or any place subject to their jurisdiction.

INSTRUCTION "C"

(After applicant has read, not aloud, the foregoing excerpts from the Constitution, he will answer the following questions in writing and without assistance:)

---

1. In case the president is unable to perform the duties of his office, who assumes them? _____

2. "Involuntary servitude" is permitted in the United States upon conviction of a crime. (True or False)_____

3. If a state is a party to a case, the constitution provides that original jurisdiction shall be in_____

4. Congress passes laws regulating cases which are included in those over which the United States Supreme Court has_____

_____ jurisdiction.

I hereby certify that I have received no assistance in the completion of this citizenship and literacy test, that I was allowed the time I desired to complete it, and that I waive any right existing to demand a copy of same. (If for any reason the applicant does not wish to sign this, he must discuss the matter with the board of registrars.)

Signed: _____
(Applicant)

The National Association for Advancement of Colored People (NAACP), established in 1909, began pursuing voter rights through the court system. In 1915 in *Guinn v. United States* the Supreme Court unanimously ruled that grandfather clauses were unconstitutional. This was the first such discriminatory voting rule to be held unconstitutional. Oklahoma had argued that no violation of section 1 of the Fifteenth Amendment existed because race was not mentioned as a qualification in its state amendment allowing grandfather clauses. The Court, however, stated that grandfather clauses perpetuated (continued) "the very condition which the Amendment was intended to destroy." Voting equality, the Court said, is not based on whether a person's grandfather was free or a slave. Despite the end of grandfather clauses, literacy tests continued. Decades later in *Lassiter v. Northampton County Board of Elections* (1959) the Court further affirmed that states can legally impose requirements to determine who is qualified to vote as long as the requirements do not discriminate as to race, color, or previous servitude. Such requirements can include age, residence, and criminal record.

Knocking down the legal barriers to the right to vote for African Americans proved less difficult than knocking down the social barriers.
Courtesy of the Library of Congress.

White-only primaries

With the loss of grandfather clauses, white-only primaries arrived as the next barrier raised to block black voters. Even if a black American passed the literacy tests and gained the right to vote in the early twentieth century, his vote was usually insignificant due to his inability to participate in primary elections. Under laws adopted by most southern states, political parties could set their own rules for membership in their party. The pro–equal rights Republican Party was essentially nonexistent in the South and the Democratic Party organized in each state as private clubs excluding all blacks. Only members, all white, of the Democratic Party were allowed to vote for candidates in its primaries. Because the Democratic Party overwhelmingly dominated in the South, whoever won in the Democratic primaries would readily win the general election. Any black votes cast in the general election were, therefore, usually meaningless.

Cases challenging the practice of white-only primaries began reaching the Supreme Court, but they brought little relief for black voters. In 1927 the Court in *Nixon v. Herndon* did ban state-approved white primaries. But in reaction, the political parties broke their formal connections with the states and the white-only primaries continued. When challenged, the Court unanimously ruled in *Grovey v. Townsend* (1935) that because the political parties had become private clubs of volunteers and were no longer a part of state government, their actions were not restricted by the Constitution.

Some progress was made in *United States v. Classic* (1941) where the Court first recognized that the primaries were increasingly becoming a key part of the formal state election process. Three years later in the landmark case of *Smith v. Allwright* (1944), the Court, using section 1 of the Fifteenth Amendment, held that voting in primary elections was a right protected by the Constitution. Primaries were viewed as state-approved elections. The earlier *Grovey* decision was reversed and private white-only primaries were considered unconstitutional. The decision was later reaffirmed in *Terry v. Adams* (1953) finally putting an end to white-only primaries. According to the court, the Fifteenth Amendment guarantee established a national policy against voting discrimination involving all elections determining national policy or selecting public officials at the national, state, or local levels. Even when private organizations act in place of the state, they are subject to constitutional restrictions.

Poll tax

With the decline of white-only primaries, another common barrier to black and poor white voters arrived in the form of the poll tax, a fee charged at polling (voting) places. The poll tax, like grandfather clauses and literacy tests, was another attempt to avoid Fifteenth Amendment violations on the basis that it was applied to blacks and whites alike.

In the late eighteenth century, the poll tax was widely considered a legitimate way to raise government revenue. By the mid-nineteenth century, with blacks unable to vote anyway, poll taxes had grown unpopular and disappeared. Their popularity returned by the early twentieth century as some states began to see poll taxes as a means to exclude blacks from the political process. Many black Americans could not afford to pay the tax. The Court in *Breedlove v. Suttles* (1937) upheld the poll tax as consistent with section 1 of the Fifteenth Amendment because it was applied to black and white voters. Public opinion again grew against the tax in the 1940s. But it wasn't until 1964 that Congress was able to pass and the states ratify the Twenty-Fourth Amendment, which abolished the poll tax in federal elections. For a brief period, states continued to impose poll taxes for state and local elections. Then the Court in *Harper v. Virginia State Board of Elections* (1966) finally struck down all poll taxes, basing its decision on the Fourteenth Amendment's equal protection clause, not the Fifteenth Amendment.

Voting districts

As the earlier barriers to voting were gradually eliminated by court decisions, an increasing number of black Americans were able to vote. A new form of barrier, manipulating voting districts, was devised to control the effectiveness of the black vote. In the United States, each county, ward, or township is divided into voting districts called precincts. Eligible voters can only vote in the precinct in which they live. Election officials verify that the voters live in the precinct and count the votes after the polls close. Therefore, how voting district boundaries are drawn greatly influences who may vote in a particular precinct. District boundaries could be redrawn by state legislatures to split up the black vote so as to make it ineffective.

The issue of changing, or redrawing, voting district boundaries came under court scrutiny in *Gomillion v. Lightfoot* (1960). The Court ruled that voting districts redrawn to ensure white political domination violated the Fifteenth Amendment. However, when the Court issued its landmark voting rights decision in *Baker v. Carr* (1962) it relied more heavily on the Fourteenth Amendment's equal protection clause in ruling that federal courts could hear cases challenging how legislative voting districts are drawn. The Court in *Baker* ruled that the Fifteenth Amendment applied

THE COURT'S NARROW VIEW
OF VOTING RIGHTS

Immediately upon ratification of the Fifteenth Amendment in 1870, Congress used its newly granted authority to pass the Enforcement Act of 1870. Section 2 of the act required that local elections be conducted without regard to race, color, or previous condition of servitude, similar wording to the Fifteenth Amendment. Section 3 prohibited the refusal to count votes of voters.

In Kentucky, a state electoral official refused to count the vote of a black American in a municipal election. The official was arrested and charged with violating the enforcement act. The case of *United States v. Reese* went to the Supreme Court and was argued in January 1875.

More than a year after arguments, the Court ruled in March 1876 that section 3 of the act was invalid because it did not specifically refer to people of color as section 2 had. Consequently, the Court held that Congress had not followed the intent of the Fifteenth, and, therefore,

more appropriately to issues involving false counts of black voter ballots, stuffing ballot boxes, or ignoring ballots from certain black voter precincts.

Section 2: Enforcement by Appropriate Legislation

Immediately following ratification, Congress exercised its newly granted powers under section 2 of the Fifteenth Amendment by passing the Enforcement Act of 1870. The act prohibited any governmental or private actions that interfere with rights guaranteed under the Fourteenth and Fifteenth amendments.

However, the courts interpreted Congress's authority in section 2 of the amendment very narrowly (limited meaning or effect). The first case involving voting rights and the enforcement act under the Fifteenth Amendment was *United States v. Reese* (1876). In the case, which involved a Kentucky municipal election, the Court not only ruled that the amendment did not apply to state and local elections but also held that the amendment did not actually grant a right to vote. Rather, it merely banned racial discrimination in voting requirements. The Court held that had exceeded its authority under the amendment. The Court stated that the amendment did not establish a right to vote, but rather only addressed the issue of racial discrimination related to voting, that is, citizens could not be excluded from voting on racial grounds.

The decision represented the Court's position of primarily applying the amendment to federal elections, and taking very narrow interpretations of congressional powers to enforce the amendment in state and local elections. Because of the *Reese* decision, the Fifteenth Amendment initially had far less impact on U.S. society than it could have. The ruling opened the door to southern states to deny voting opportunities to black Americans through means such as literacy tests and white-only primaries in state and local elections through the first half of the twentieth century. Congress repealed other sections of the enforcement act in 1894. One section of the ill-fated act did live on: the prohibition of conspiracies by private people to block citizens from enjoying their constitutional rights. Through time this basic prohibition was broadened to include all rights and privileges granted under the Constitution. It persisted through the twentieth century.

the amendment did "not confer the right [to vote] ... upon any one" but rather provided "the citizens of the United States with a new constitutional right which is ... exemption [freedom] from discrimination in the exercise of elective franchise on account of race, color, or previous condition of servitude." In another court decision that year, *United States v. Cruikshank* (1876), the Court reemphasized that the federal government was responsible for protecting citizens from racial discrimination in voting and the states determine who has the right to vote.

These narrow interpretations of the Fifteenth left it open to the states to devise all types of barriers, such as grandfather clauses, literacy tests, and all white primaries, to discourage black voters through the next several decades.

One of the few Court Decisions favorable to the Fifteenth Amendment came in *ex parte Yarbrough* (1884). In that case the Court upheld the convictions of Ku Klux Klan members who blocked a black man's attempt to vote in a federal congressional election. This ruling proved an exception in upholding federal authority over the actions of private individuals during the late nineteenth century. Justice Samuel F. Miller

(1816–1890) wrote that the Fifteenth Amendment does "substantially confer on the Negro the right to vote." This broader interpretation of the Fifteenth was largely ignored in later rulings.

Momentum builds

For more than a half-century, the narrow interpretations of Congress's power in section 2 prevailed, and no major laws protecting black voting rights were passed. The Civil Rights movement beginning in the 1950s dramatically increased public awareness of racial discrimination in America. Congress passed civil rights acts in 1957 and 1960, although they were not as strong concerning the black vote as many believed they should have been. The 1957 Civil Rights Act prohibited private acts of intimidation or coercion that interfered with citizens voting in federal elections. The act also gave the U.S. attorney general power to obtain injunctions (court orders to stop certain actions) against discriminatory acts by private parties regardless of the nature of the election. The 1960 Civil Rights Act expanded the attorney general's authority beyond specific individual incidents. The act gave the attorney general authority to identify areas where patterns of voter discrimination were occurring and, if needed, authorized the use of court-appointed officials to guide voter registration in those areas.

These new attorney general powers were upheld and expanded by the Court in several rulings. For example, the Court in *United States v. Raines* (1960) ruled state election officials were subject to Fifteenth Amendment prohibitions on racial discrimination. Then a *United States v. Mississippi* (1965) ruling supported the attorney general's authority under the civil rights acts to sue state election officials for Fifteenth Amendment violations.

In general, however, court rulings involving voting rights still remained narrow. The Court in *Harman v. Forssenius* (1965) ruled that even though the right to vote for a candidate of choice is a fundamental right and the essence of a democratic society with a representative government, the Fifteenth Amendment did not protect people from *private* discriminatory conduct. With this continued weak application of the Fifteenth, understanding tests grew in popularity in the South to restrict black votes. The tests applied by states required voter applicants to show that they understood and could explain sections of the state or federal constitution selected by the testing official. The standards for selecting the sections individuals should explain and for grading the results were very subjective (open to individual interpretation) and often discriminatory. When challenged, the Court in *Louisiana v. United States* (1965) banned subjectively applied understanding tests. The Court also required that any new tests devised by a state must be given to all its voters, not just new ones, to guarantee the same standards were being applied to all.

Congress passes major voting rights law

In March 1965, Dr. Martin Luther King, Jr., (1929–1968) led a march of 3,200 black protesters and white sympathizers from Selma to Montgomery, Alabama, to protest denial of voting rights to blacks. The public was greatly alarmed by Alabama state troopers assaulting a peaceful voting rights march. Congress took action and passed the Voting Rights Act of 1965, largely founded on authority of section 2 of the Fifteenth Amendment. Campaigning for passage of the act, President Lyndon B. Johnson (1908–1994) told a joint session of Congress, "Unless the right to vote be secured and undenied, all other rights are insecure and subject to denial for all citizens. The challenge of this right is a challenge to America itself." The 1965 act, expanding on the prohibitions of the previous civil rights acts, revolutionized southern politics. Congress had finally effectively exercised its authority to protect the voting rights of minorities almost a full century after adoption of the Fifteen Amendment.

The act initially focused on seven southern states (Alabama, Georgia, Louisiana, Mississippi, North Carolina, South Carolina, and Virginia) and outlawed restrictive voting requirements that denied the right of a U.S. citizen to vote because of race, color, or membership in a language minority group. A target of the act was any "device" associated with a requirement to test reading, writing, comprehension, or interpretation skills, or to demonstrate a certain knowledge or determine good moral character. It gave courts the authority to review election districts that were accused of racial discrimination. It also required the use of smaller voting districts to improve representation of blacks.

The act prohibited literacy tests in federal, state, local, general, and primary elections in any state or county where voter registration was particularly low. In certain counties, federal officials became responsible for guiding voter registration to ensure fairness in determining voter eligibility. The act also required the seven states to obtain federal approval before making any changes to their election systems such as relocating polling sites, changing ballot forms, and altering voting districts. For example, any changes in voting districts had to receive approval of the U.S. attorney general or U.S. district court to make sure the reapportionment "does not have the purpose and will not have the effect of denying ... the right to vote on account of race or color."

Fifteenth Amendment

CIVIL RIGHTS MOVEMENT

Although landmark Supreme Court decisions in constitutional law often inspire changes to longstanding injustices in American society, sometimes public events lead to major change where congressional action or a court decision could not. Perhaps one of the more dramatic examples of private citizens influencing constitutional law was the drive by black Americans for equal voting rights.

Despite passage of the Fifteenth Amendment in 1870 that established voting rights for black citizens, little progress in freedom to exercise voting rights occurred for the next ninety years. Improved prospects for change came in 1954 when the U.S. Supreme Court issued its *Brown v. Board of Education of Topeka, Kansas* landmark decision striking down segregation in public elementary schools. However, it was evident that black activism was necessary to force the government to extend racial reform in *Brown* to other aspects of life. What is referred to as the Civil Rights movement was born. The movement represented a "freedom struggle" by black Americans to gain equality with white Americans and freedom from discrimination including equal opportunity in employment, education, and housing, the right to vote, and equal access to public facilities.

A series of events soon unfolded that defined the movement. In December 1955, Rosa Parks was arrested in Montgomery, Alabama, for refusing to give her seat on a city bus to a white man as required by city law. A rally in support of Parks was held at the Holt Street Baptist Church. A 27-year-old preacher named Martin Luther King, Jr., attended. King gave an inspirational speech calling for nonviolent, civil disobedience (peacefully not obeying certain laws) in contrast to the Ku Klux Klan which used violence. By late 1956, the Supreme Court ruled the Montgomery bus law unconstitutional.

Voting rights act challenged

Southern states considered the 1965 Voting Rights Act an attack on states' rights (strong state legal powers as opposed to federal powers) and soon the act was challenged in the courts. The resulting landmark decision came in *South Carolina v. Katzenbach* (1966) in which the Supreme Court ruled the act was consistent with Congress's power under section 2 of the Fifteenth Amendment to eliminate racial discrimination in voting.

With momentum established, King founded the Southern Christian Leadership Conference (SCLC) in 1957 to provide leadership to the movement. The high point of the Civil Rights movement occurred on August 28, 1963, when 250,000 people participated in a march on Washington urging the federal government to support desegregation (end of racial separation in public places) and protect voting rights. King gave his famous "I Have a Dream" speech calling for nonviolent direct action and voter registration. Congress responded with passage of the Civil Rights Act of 1964. Though sweeping in prohibiting discrimination in public accommodations such as hotels, theaters, buses, and railroad cars, the act did not address voting rights.

A campaign grew to register black voters throughout the South. In response, white violence escalated. Medgar Evers, a black leader, was shot and killed in Jackson, Mississippi, while organizing a boycott protesting voter discrimination. In June 1964, three students, two of them white, who were promoting voter registration were murdered in Mississippi. That shocked the nation. In 1965, King led a march protesting voting restrictions from Selma to Montgomery, Alabama. After first being attacked by mounted police using tear gas and clubs, the march was finally held with court permission. More than twenty-five thousand people joined the march. They were protected by three thousand federal troops. Congress responded with the Voting Rights Act of 1965. The act expanded blacks' voting rights by prohibiting use of literacy tests and other forms of discriminatory qualifications. The act gave oversight of state voting laws to the federal government.

King, who received the Nobel Peace Prize in 1964 for his leadership role in the movement, was assassinated in Memphis, Tennessee, in 1968. With its leader gone and unity no longer evident, the Civil Rights movement's national thrust faded. No other twentieth century social movement had as profound an effect on U.S. political and legal institutions.

Expanding on the act, the Court outlined broad congressional powers to enforce the Fifteenth Amendment. Congress could even decide whether a certain region of the nation had widespread voter discrimination and focus on correcting that region. Such an area could be where low minority voting registration rates were present and registration tests are applied.

Within a few years, the rise in black voter registration was dramatic. In Mississippi alone, black registration rose to almost 60 percent by

*In 1984, Jesse
Jackson was the
first African
American to ever
win a significant
number of delegates
in the run to be
the Democratic
Party's candidate
for President
of the United
States. He won
even more delegates
in the 1988 race.*

Reproduced by permission
of Rev. Jesse Jackson.

1968. Challenges to literacy tests continued. In *Gaston County v. United
States* (1969) the Court ruled that past discrimination in the educational
system might make the use of literacy tests in certain areas inappropriate.
In 1970 Congress, under its section 2 authority, suspended use of literacy
tests nationwide for five years. The Court upheld this suspension in *Oregon v. Mitchell* (1970).

Revisions in 1975 and 1982 expanded the voting rights act. The
changes required that election materials be provided in languages other
than English in certain areas. Passage of the National Voter Registration
Act of 1993, supported by the National Association for the Advancement

of Colored Persons (NAACP), eliminated the restrictive voter registration requirements. Citizens may register to vote when applying for a state driver's license or register at a polling place with a driver's license and two personal witnesses.

Congress's powers expanded

Other Court decisions related to the Fifteenth Amendment followed, further expanding Congress's powers under section 2. *Hadnott v. Amos* (1969) even addressed *candidate* rights under the Fifteenth Amendment by declaring candidate requirements cannot be based on race. In *City of Richmond v. United States* (1975) the Court ruled that state attempts to discriminate against blacks are unconstitutional regardless of whether discrimination actually occurs.

The Court ruled in *City of Rome v. United States* (1980) that although an intent to discriminate might be necessary to prove a violation of section 1, Congress had the power under section 2 to prohibit all electoral practices that result in discrimination regardless of whether they were intended. Congress only has to prove a legitimate purpose for a voting law to be constitutionally acceptable under section 2 of the amendment. By the end of the twentieth century, general federal oversight of state voting policies had become widely acceptable.

Summing the Parts of the Fifteenth Amendment

In addressing the voting rights of citizens, section 1 of the Fifteenth Amendment authorized courts to strike down state laws that denied voting rights due to race. Section 2 gave Congress broad powers to pass laws enforcing section 1's ban on racial discrimination in voting. However, congressional efforts to enforce the amendment were immediately met with adverse Supreme Court rulings. For almost a century, state legislatures in the South and elsewhere adopted a series of different measures designed to limit the black vote. Finally, influenced by the Civil Rights movement, Congress took more assertive steps in ending discriminatory voting practices, making it easier for blacks to register and vote.

The Voting Rights Act in 1965, passed under its authority of section 2 of the Fifteenth Amendment, for the first time gave the federal government power traditionally left to the states to operate election processes. Passage of the 1965 act broke down voting barriers, leading to significantly higher voter registration levels among blacks and eventually to the election of many black Americans to public offices in areas previously dominated by whites.

For More Information

Books

Clayton, Dewey M. *African Americans and the Politics of Congressional Redistricting.* New York: Garland Publications, 2000.

Guiner, Lani. *The Tyranny of the Majority: Fundamental Fairness in Representative Democracy.* New York: Free Press, 1994.

Mathews, John Mabry. *Legislative and Judicial History of the Fifteenth Amendment.* New York: DaCapo Press, 1971.

Nieman, Donald G. *Black Southerners and the Law, 1865–1900.* New York: Garland Publications, 1994.

Rush, Mark E. *Voting Rights and Redistricting in the United States.* Westport, CT: Greenwood Press, 1998.

Web sites

Findlaw Internet Legal Resources. *The Fifteenth Amendment and Annotations.* [Online] http://caselaw.findlaw.com/data/constitution/amendment15/01.html (accessed July 28, 2000)

FindLaw Internet Legal Resources. *U.S. Supreme Court Opinions.* [Online] http://www.findlaw.com/casecode/supreme.html (accessed on July 28, 2000).

Library of Congress's African American Odyssey Exhibit Web site—Slavery—The Peculiar Institution. [Online] http://lcweb2.loc.gov/ammem/aaohtml/exhibit/aopart1.html (accessed September 17, 2000)

Sources

Books

Biskupic, Joan, and Elder Witt. *Guide to the U.S. Supreme Court.* 3rd ed. Washington, DC: Congressional Quarterly, 1997.

Hall, Kermit L., ed. *Oxford Companion to the Supreme Court of the United States.* New York: Oxford University Press, 1992.

Stephens, Otis H., Jr., and John M. Schebb II. *American Constitutional Law.* St. Paul, MN: West Publishing, 1993.

West's Encyclopedia of American Law. St. Paul, MN: West Group, 1999.

Sixteenth Amendment

The Congress shall have the power to lay and collect taxes on incomes, from whatever source derived, without apportionment among the several States, and without regard to any census or enumeration.

The Sixteenth Amendment grants Congress the right to place a tax on the incomes of both individuals and corporations. Before the amendment, Congress had the right to levy taxes on states, but not on individuals. Article I, Section 10 of the Constitution states that all taxes must be apportioned (divided up) among the states. This meant that each state had to be taxed equally. Adjustments were made for states with larger or smaller populations, but, in general, Congress did not have the constitutional right to tax individuals. Only states had the right under the Constitution to tax their citizens. Therefore, for Congress to levy a national individual income tax, the Constitution had to be amended.

Origins of the Sixteenth Amendment

The idea of a graduated income tax was not new when it was submitted to Congress in 1909. For centuries, churches and other religious organizations had asked members to give a percentage of their income. This donation of part of one's income (often 10 percent) was called tithing, and enabled members to give according to their ability.

During the Middle Ages, some rulers in Italy collected a tax on incomes. From 1799 to 1816, the British Parliament set up a temporary income tax to finance their wars against Napoleon Bonaparte (1769–1821). (Napolean was the French emperor who was waging war against much of Europe and the Mediterranean countries at that time.) The British finally started a permanent income tax in 1874.

Sixteenth
Amendment

RATIFICATION FACTS

PROPOSED: Submitted by Congress to the states on July 12, 1909.

RATIFICATION: Ratified by the required three-fourths of states (thirty-six of forty-eight) on February 3, 1913. Declared to be part of the Constitution on February 25, 1913.

RATIFYING STATES: Alabama, August 10, 1909; Kentucky, February 8, 1910; South Carolina, February 19, 1910; Illinois, March 1, 1910; Mississippi, March 7, 1910; Oklahoma, March 10, 1910; Maryland, April 8, 1910; Georgia, August 3, 1910; Texas, August 16, 1910; Ohio, January 19, 1911; Idaho, January 20, 1911; Oregon, January 23, 1911; Washington, January 26, 1911; Montana, January 30, 1911; Indiana, January 30, 1911; California, January 31, 1911; Nevada, January 31, 1911; South Dakota, February 3, 1911; Nebraska, February 9, 1911; North Carolina, February 11, 1911; Colorado, February 15, 1911; North Dakota, February 17, 1911; Kansas, February 18, 1911; Michigan, February 23, 1911; Iowa, February 24, 1911; Missouri, March 16, 1911; Maine, March 31, 1911; Tennessee, April 7, 1911; Arkansas, April 22, 1911 (after having rejected it earlier); Wisconsin, May 26, 1911; New York, July 12, 1911; Arizona, April 6, 1912; Minnesota, June 11, 1912; Louisiana, June 28, 1912; West Virginia, January 31, 1913; New Mexico, February 3, 1913.

In the United States, the first income tax appeared as the Civil War Income Tax of 1862. The United States was engaged in the Civil War (1861–65), and it was turning out to be a very expensive conflict. Salmon P. Chase, the Secretary of the Treasury at the time, came up with the idea of taxing incomes as an evenhanded way of dividing up the expense of the war.

Many states had adopted income tax as a temporary measure to pay the cost of the war. Secretary Chase's plan was also meant to be temporary. The income tax he envisioned would raise money, and involve individual citizens in the war effort. Secretary Chase's tax was a graduated tax that included a six hundred dollar exemption, meaning that a taxpayer did not have to pay tax on the first six hundred dollars of his or her income. Six hundred dollars was a lot of money in 1862, but Secretary Chase persuaded citizens to accept his tax proposal by assuring them that only the very wealthy would end up paying much money.

3 2 0   *C o n s t i t u t i o n a l   A m e n d m e n t s*

Why tax incomes?

Setting up an income tax was an attempt to make taxation more fair. The idea behind taxing incomes was that those who made more money would pay more tax. Those who earned less money would pay little or no income tax. This type of taxation is called a progressive, or graduate, tax.

A regressive tax (also known as sales tax) is one where everyone pays the same percentage of the cost of goods. Regressive taxes are harder on poor people, because it eats up a big portion of a small income. (As opposed to taking a little bite out of a large income.) For example, a 5 percent sales tax on a $100 item adds $5 to the price of the item. To a cashier at a fast food restaurant, $5 might represent an hour of work. A lawyer who charges $250 an hour would hardly notice an additional $5.

A progressive income tax allows someone with a low income to pay a smaller percentage than someone with a higher income. The percentage to be paid increases in steps, or what is known as "income brackets." A progressive tax allows a person to pay what they can. To many, this is more fair than a regressive tax that would expect everyone to pay the same amount regardless of their income.

Citizens did not appreciate the tax collector any more than they appreciated the taxes. Reproduced by permission of Archive Photos, Inc.

Sixteenth Amendment

BEFORE INCOME TAXES

In the early days of the United States, there were few taxes. In fact, until 1817 there were no internal taxes at all. The new U.S. government raised the money it needed by adding taxes onto the price of goods. Taxes on imported goods are called tariffs, and taxes on domestic goods are called excise taxes. Governments still charge tariffs and excise taxes today.

Tariffs raise revenue (income) for the government, but they also serve another purpose—to raise the price of imported goods. Items imported from other countries are often cheaper than those produced in the United States. Adding a tariff increases the price of the imported goods, and helps domestically produced products compete with them. In the 1700s and 1800s, tariffs caused disagreements among people in different parts of the country.

In the North, there were many factories that produced consumer goods (like woven cloth or farm tools). The factory owners were happy about the tariffs. Tariffs made the price of imports go up. Raised prices let northern made products compete with imports. Even the workers in the factories benefited. If more people bought domestically produced goods, there were more factory jobs.

In the West and South, on the other hand, people depended on farming. They got no benefit from the higher prices of imported manufactured goods. They did not work in the factories that made manufactured goods, nor did they sell the goods. They only bought them. Using tariffs to raise the prices on imported products did not do the farmers any good at all.

Creating a New Kind of Tax

The Income Tax Act of 1862 set up a Bureau of Internal Revenue, with a commissioner of internal revenue at its head. The commissioner assessed and collected income taxes. He enforced the new tax by prosecuting those who refused to pay by taking their money or property as payment.

In 1862, people were taxed in much the same way they are now. Those who made less than six hundred dollars per year paid no tax. Above six hundred dollars, there were tax "brackets" that corresponded

However, even certain goods produced in the United States were taxed with an added fee called an excise tax. Excise taxes were a kind of sales tax. They were often placed on luxury items, like tobacco, alcohol, sugar, and snuff. The excise tax began in seventeenth century Holland, and was used in Dutch colonies in the Americas, like New York. Excise taxes were soon widely used by governments to raise money throughout both Europe and the colonies. Later, it was used by the United States when it was formed.

While the federal government used tariffs and excise taxes to raise money, state governments used another kind of tax: the property tax. A property tax charged a fee to those who owned land. The more the land was worth, the higher the tax charged. The property tax was a progressive tax that was fair in more ways than the tariffs and excise taxes.

Tariffs and excise taxes were regressive taxes that just added a flat fee to certain items. This increased their price the same amount for both rich and poor. The property tax was considered more fair because wealthier people usually owned more valuable property. Therefore, they paid more taxes than the poor.

However, taxing property created a division between those who lived on farms and ranches, and those who lived in the cities. In the mid-1800s, the Industrial Revolution started. More and more factories were built in cities. Factories drew people in from the countryside to work in the new manufacturing jobs. Factory workers became urban dwellers who rented rather than owning property—and consequently didn't pay property taxes. The farmers and other rural landowners felt it was unfair to tax their property, especially since the factory workers and owners paid few taxes on the money they made.

to different levels of income—the higher your income, the higher your tax. Wealthy people who made over $10 thousand a year paid a flat 3 percent tax on their incomes.

Even such a limited income tax was very effective in raising money. However, the Income Tax Act of 1862 was only a temporary law designed so that the United States could pay off its enormous Civil War debts. When the act expired in 1870, there was much debate over whether to renew the income tax.

Sixteenth Amendment

Wealthy people favored other kinds of taxation. A small excise tax on tobacco or a tariff on imported goods did not affect them very much. A tax on their rising incomes did. However, poor and working middle class people thought that an income tax was a fair way to raise money. The poor did not actually get money from the taxes on the rich, but they did get more services from the government. Walking the tightrope between these two positions, Congress passed limited income tax bills in 1870 and 1871. In 1872, the wealthy business owners finally won the debate, and the income tax lapsed.

Income Tax and the Populist Party

After the Civil War, farmers and other rural dwellers from the West and South felt more and more that their interests were being overlooked in favor of the industrialists from the big cities that were largely in the North. They formed "Farmer's Alliances"—groups where they could talk about their grievances, and make political plans.

The first Farmer's Alliance formed in 1877. A group of farmers in Texas facing hard economic times met to discuss their problems. Similar alliances soon formed all over Texas. By 1886, there were two thousand alliances with one hundred thousand members in Texas alone. Alliances also formed in Georgia, Tennessee, Kansas, the Dakotas, and other places in the rural United States.

By the 1890s, the farmers' situation was becoming more and more desperate. The prices for equipment and goods they needed to buy were going up, but the prices they could get for their crops were going down. In 1891, representatives from the various state alliances met in a national convention in Cincinnati, Ohio. By 1892, members of the farmer's alliances were so disgusted with the prevailing parties (Republican and Democrat) that they met again in Omaha, Nebraska, and picked their own candidate for president.

The Populist, or People's, Party, as they now called themselves, wanted to change many things, but their major goal was "to restore the government of the Republic to the hands of the 'plain people,' the class with which it originated." They also wanted: to reform currency by minting more coins and printing more paper money; to elect U.S. senators by direct vote of the people (see the Seventeenth Amendment); to institute an eight-hour work day; to establish pensions; to begin immigration reform; as well as to reform (change) other laws. They also wanted a progressive, graduated income tax.

The Populist movement was so powerful that it began to make the other major parties take note of their demands. In the 1892 presidential election, James Weaver was the Populists first candidate for president. He won over one million votes. During this same election, the Democratic Party took on some of the Populists most important issues. Among them, the income tax.

In 1894, William Jennings Bryan, a Democratic congressional representative from Nebraska, designed a simple 2 percent income tax on all income over $4 thousand per year. Bryan was a persuasive speaker, and gave a dramatic speech to support his tax bill. "Of all the mean [cheap] men I have ever known," he said, "I have never known one so mean that I would be willing to say of him that his patriotism was less than 2 percent deep!" Bryan's tax bill passed.

The Populists transferred most of their support to the Democrats and faded from sight as a political force. However, their influence is seen in much of the liberal legislation of the late nineteenth and early twentieth centuries. One such piece of legislation is the Sixteenth Amendment.

Heading Toward an Amendment

The victory of the 1894 tax bill was short lived. Determined to fight the government's taxing of their incomes, many wealthy people and corporations sued the government for charging this tax. They claimed that the new tax was unconstitutional, and said it violated Article I, section 10 of the Constitution. This section states that all taxes must be distributed equally among all the states. On May 20, 1895, the United States Supreme Court agreed, and ruled that the income tax was unconstitutional.

This was when Congress realized that the Constitution would have to be amended before an income tax could be instituted. Because so many people felt strongly about the tax and how it should be implemented, it took a long time to come up with an amendment that Congress could even agree to propose. Thirty-three different amendments were suggested and rejected for one reason or another before the final wording was approved by Congress in 1909.

After Congress approved the proposed amendment, it was time to send it to the states for ratification. The amendment passed quickly in the South and West where the income tax had always been popular. Things took longer in the industrialized North. But, by the end of February, 1913, Delaware became the thirty-sixth state to ratify the Sixteenth

Sixteenth Amendment

You can be arrested for failing to pay your taxes. Mobster Al Capone was jailed on tax evasion. Reproduced by permission of Archive Photos, Inc.

Amendment, the last state needed to make the amendment part of the U.S. Constitution. William Howard Taft (1857–1930) was president when Congress approved the amendment, but it was Woodrow Wilson (1856–1924) who signed it into law. He ended the long process that had first started in 1895.

Taxing crime

The first act based on the Sixteenth Amendment included the words "lawful business" to describe the kind of income taxable under the new law. In 1921, Congress passed the Revenue Act of 1921. This act removed the word "lawful," and allowed the government to tax *all* income—even that from illegal enterprises. The first case to test this new taxation on illegal businesses was *United States vs. Sullivan* (1927).

Manly S. Sullivan was a businessman who sold illegal liquor. He was caught, and prosecuted for his crime, but he hoped to avoid an additional charge of tax evasion. He claimed that since the Fifth Amendment gave him the right not to incriminate himself (that is, not to accuse himself of a crime), he did not have to publicly admit his illegal income in order to pay taxes on it. The Supreme Court, under Chief Justice Oliver Wendell

Holmes, disagreed with Sullivan's argument. The Court ruled that he was required to pay taxes on the money he received from his illegal business.

Probably the most famous tax evasion case involving someone in illegal business was that of Al Capone. Capone was a notorious gangster in the 1920s who ran much of Chicago's illegal business. The Federal Bureau of Investigation (FBI) estimated his $105 million income in 1927 came from illegal activities such as selling alcohol, prostitution, and gambling. However, the FBI was unable to gather enough evidence to prosecute him for those crimes. Instead, Capone was finally caught and convicted of income tax evasion, and was sentenced to eleven years in prison.

The Tax that Grew and Grew

Though several different Congresses had fought, argued, and worked hard to pass an income tax amendment, the early income tax only accounted for a small part of the federal government's revenue. This was partly due to a low tax rate, and partly to a high exemption (the amount of income not subject to taxation).

The 1913 income tax was the first under the new amendment. It taxed people with an income over three thousand dollars, four thousand dollars for married couples. The lowest taxable income rate was 1 percent; the highest rate was 7 percent (on incomes over five hundred thousand dollars). In 1918, income taxes collected from U.S. citizens amounted to over $1 billion for the first time. By 1920, the figure was $5.4 billion.

Until 1943, there was not a dependable way to assess how much income tax people owed and no effective way to collect that tax. The system depended largely on voluntary compliance. Even if people had every intention of paying, poor and low-income working people often did not have enough extra money to pay their tax bills.

In 1943, the United States became involved in World War II (1939–44). There were many expenses that went along with waging war, and lawmakers searched for ways to increase revenues from income tax. The idea they came up with was called "withholding." This meant that money for taxes was taken out of a person's pay, and was sent to the government before the person received their paycheck. President Franklin Roosevelt vetoed Congress's proposal for withholding taxes. He felt that it would be too hard on low-income people, but the law passed anyway.

Withholding taxes greatly increased the number of people paying taxes. For example, in 1935 there were 4 million taxpayers. Just ten years

*During World War I,
income tax dollars
helped support the
United States armed
forces.* Reproduced by
permission of AP/Wide
World Photos.

later, in 1945, the number of taxpayers climbed to 42.7 million. The revenue from income tax also rose. They rose from $1 billion in 1918, to $43 billion by 1943. By 1999, income tax revenues ballooned to $508.4 billion, and showed no signs of decreasing.

Ever since the Civil War Income Tax of 1862, politicians have persuaded the American people to accept the income tax. They have assured them that, with low percentages and high exemptions, it would effect only the richest taxpayers. Withholding changed all that. What started as a fairly minor tax that mostly affected the wealthy had become everybody's tax.

The Ever-Changing Tax Code

Amending the Constitution to allow an income tax was just the start of creating the modern American income tax. The Internal Revenue Code, also called the U.S. Tax Code, is the book of laws that actually spells out the details of the income tax. While the Sixteenth Amendment gave Congress the right to ask citizens to pay an income tax, it is the Tax Code laws that determine exactly how to implement that tax.

The Code has been expanded and changed many times, and is now over 2,000 pages long. The Tax Code explains in detail exactly which income is taxable, and at what rate. It also outlines which expenses and purchases taxpayers can deduct from their income in order to lower their taxes. These laws are very complicated, because they need to describe in detail every deduction, credit, subsidy, and exemption. In fact, tax laws and forms are so complex that in 1991, 40 percent of all taxpayers hired professional tax people to do their taxes for them.

Other ways to use the Tax Code

MAKE IT SIMPLE WITH A FLAT TAX. Many taxpayers feel that the Tax Code is just too complex and must be simplified. One suggestion that politicians have offered is the "flat tax." The flat tax is the opposite of a graduated tax. Instead of paying a percentage of one's income that gradually increases as one earns more, all taxpayers would pay the same "flat" tax rate. This might simplify the process of paying taxes, but many argue that it would remove the basic fairness of the graduated income tax: that those who earn more pay a higher percentage.

USING THE TAX CODE FOR FINANCIAL "REWARDS." The Tax Code has another interesting function. Lawmakers can actually use the tax code to encourage people to make certain decisions in their lives. For instance, people who own houses are allowed to deduct part of the cost of buying their house from their income so that they pay less tax. There is not a similar deduction for those who rent a house or apartment. In this way, the government encourages people to become homeowners, and financially rewards them for buying a house. There are many ways the government can use the financial reward of a tax deduction to enforce the government's own values, or to help business.

Over the years, the Tax Code has been changed to reflect the political atmosphere of the times. In 1982 for example, a conservative Republican administration led the way to large tax cuts for the wealthiest individuals and

corporations. The tax rate for the highest income brackets was cut from 70 percent to 50 percent. The Tax Reform Act of 1986 continued to cut even more, and the rate dropped from 50 percent to 28 percent—much lower than the original 70 percent. On the other side, in the mid-1990s, a more liberal Democratic administration increased the Earned Income Credit, which is a payment from the government to help very low income taxpayers.

The Tax We Love to Hate

The Civil War Income Tax of 1862 was first introduced in the United States as a fairly small tax to increase the country's income during the war. Even after the Sixteenth Amendment legalized a permanent income tax, the income tax did not supply the largest part of the country's revenue. The nation's major source of income was from the tariffs and excise taxes that were the traditional taxes in Europe.

Hard economic times hit the United States during the 1930s, and the U.S. government depended more on income tax for raising money. With the beginning of World War II in 1941, and the introduction of income tax withholding in 1943, the importance of the income tax as the

Buying a house can earn you a credit on your federal income tax return. Reproduced by permission of AP/Wide World Photos.

FORM 1040	Department of the Treasury – Internal Revenue Service	1997			
	U.S. Individual Income Tax Return		(99)	IRS Use Only – Do not write or staple in this space.	

For the year Jan. 1 – Dec. 31, 1997, or other tax year beginning , 1997, ending , 19   OMB No. 1545-0074

Label (See instructions on page 10.) Use the IRS label. Otherwise, please print or type.

Your first name and initial: **William J.**   Last name: **Clinton**   Your social security number: ▓▓▓▓▓▓▓

If a joint return, spouse's first name and initial: **Hillary Rodham**   Last name: **Clinton**   Spouse's social security number: ▓▓▓▓▓▓▓

Home address (number and street). If you have a P.O. box, see page 10.: **1600 Pennsylvania Avenue, N.W.**   Apt. no.:

City, town or post office, state, and ZIP code. If you have a foreign address, see page 10.: **Washington, DC 20500**

For help finding line instructions, see pages 2 and 3 in the booklet.

Presidential Election Campaign (See page 10.)

	Yes	No	Note: Checking "Yes" will not change your tax or reduce your refund.
Do you want $3 to go to this fund?		X	
If a joint return, does your spouse want $3 to go to this fund?		X	

Filing Status
Check only one box.

1 Single
2 X Married filing joint return (even if only one had income)
3 Married filing separate return. Enter spouse's soc. sec. no. above & full name here ▶
4 Head of household (with qualifying person). (See page 10.) If the qualifying person is a child but not your dependent, enter this child's name here ▶
5 Qualifying widow(er) with dependent child (year spouse died ▶ 19   ). (See page 10.)

Exemptions

If more than six dependents, see page 10.

6a ☒ Yourself. If your parent (or someone else) can claim you as a dependent on his or her tax return, do not check box 6a ....
b ☒ Spouse ....

No. of boxes checked on 6a and 6b: **2**

c Dependents:

(1) First Name Last name	(2) Dependent's social security number	(3) Dependent's relationship to you	(4) No. of mos. lived in your home in 1997	
Chelsea V. Clinton	▓▓▓▓▓▓	Daughter	12	● lived with you **1**
				● did not live with you due to divorce or separation (see page 11)
				Dependents on 6c not entered above

No. of your children on 6c who:

d Total number of exemptions claimed .... Add numbers entered on lines above ▶ **3**

Income

Attach Copy B of your Forms W-2, W-2G, and 1099-R here.

If you did not get a W-2, see page 12.

Enclose, but do not attach, any payment. Also, please use Form 1040-V.

7	Wages, salaries, tips, etc. Attach Form(s) W-2	7	200,076
8a	Taxable interest. Attach Schedule B if required	8a	22,555
b	Tax-exempt interest. DO NOT include on line 8a 8b 5,458		
9	Dividends. Attach Schedule B if required	9	7,764
10	Taxable refunds, credits, or offsets of state and local income taxes (see page 12)	10	19
11	Alimony received	11	
12	Business income or (loss). Attach Schedule C or C-EZ	12	281,898
13	Capital gain or (loss). Attach Schedule D	13	65,028
14	Other gains or (losses). Attach Form 4797	14	
15a	Total IRA distributions ..... 15a b Taxable amount (see pg. 13)	15b	
16a	Total pensions and annuities 16a b Taxable amount (see pg. 13)	16b	
17	Rental real estate, royalties, partnerships, S corporations, trusts, etc. Attach Schedule E	17	1
18	Farm income or (loss). Attach Schedule F	18	
19	Unemployment compensation	19	
20a	Social security benefits ..... 20a b Taxable amount (see pg. 14)	20b	
21	Other income.	21	
22	Add the amounts in the far right column for lines 7 through 21. This is your total income ..... ▶	22	577,341

Adjusted Gross Income

If line 32 is under $29,290 (under $9,770 if a child did not live with you), see EIC inst. on page 21.

23	IRA deduction (see page 16)	23		
24	Medical savings account deduction. Attach Form 8853	24		
25	Moving expenses. Attach Form 3903 or 3903-F	25		
26	One-half of self-employment tax. Attach Schedule SE	26	7,830	
27	Self-employed health insurance deduction (see page 17)...	27		
28	Keogh and self-employed SEP and SIMPLE plans	28		
29	Penalty on early withdrawal of savings	29		
30	Alimony paid. b Recipient's SSN ▶	30a		
31	Add lines 23 through 30a		31	7,830
32	Subtract line 31 from line 22. This is your adjusted gross income .... ▶		32	569,511

For Privacy Act and Paperwork Reduction Act Notice, see page 38.   Form **1040** (1997)

Everyone has to complete federal tax return forms, which are long and complicated.

Reproduced by permission of AP/Wide World Photos.

federal government's source of income continued to increase. By 1997, income taxes collected from citizens provided 85 percent of the revenue that funds the U.S. federal government, making it even more truly a government "by the people."

When April 15—the federal due-date for taxes—rolls around each year, most taxpayers complain a lot. They may spend hours hunched over piles of complex forms with names like 1040A, 4562, and Schedules A, B, C, D, and E. Comedians on TV make jokes, and post office employees work overtime as long lines of grumpy last minute taxpayers

TAX RESISTANCE

Americans have a long history of refusing to pay taxes as a way of protesting a government's policies. The Boston Tea Party of December, 1773, was an early example of American tax resistance. Rather than paying a tax they considered unfair, patriotic colonists boarded ships and threw imported tea into the Boston harbor.

In western Massachusetts in 1786, Daniel Shays led a large group of farmers and other working people who protested harsh penalties for debts and non-payment of taxes. These tax protesters were angry enough to arm themselves and fight for better conditions. After several clashes with government militia "Shays Rebellion," as it was called, was stopped. Daniel Shays was pardoned, but more than a dozen of those who had marched with him were hanged. These kinds of public demonstration allowed protesters to publicize their cause in a dramatic way, and to gain support from other like-minded people.

The income tax is a very personal—even intrusive—tax. The government demands to know intimate details about the lives and work of taxpayers, and requires people to give the government part of their hard-earned salaries. From the time the income tax became a permanent part of American life in 1913, some have refused to pay their income tax. They are called evaders.

Some tax evaders have based their resistance solely on principle. Some have never approved of the direct connection between the people and the federal government. They believe that the federal government was never meant to have as much power as it does. They speak of the evils of what they call "big government," or an overly powerful federal government that comes in and tells the state and the individual what they must do. Some people also oppose other federally enforced programs, such as the integration of schools. One such group is the Freemen of Montana.

The Freemen came to national notice in the spring of 1996. A group of eleven Freemen occupied a ranch in Montana. They held feder-

try to get their tax returns in by the deadline. Even though many taxpayers resent sending hard-earned money to the government, all governments must collect taxes. Hopefully, citizens see the benefits of their tax payments in the services they receive from their government.

al agents off with firearms and explosives for eighty-one days before they were finally arrested. The Freemen do not believe in the authority of the United States government. They set up their own government with their own courts.

They quote parts of the United States Constitution, the Bible, and the Magna Carta (England's charter of citizens rights). They believe these documents give them the authority to act independently of the U.S. government. They refuse to engage with the government at all: they don't pay taxes, and they don't obtain driver's licenses, social security numbers, or building permits. They even refuse to use zip codes on their mail.

Another group that opposes the income tax is the Libertarian Party. Formed in 1972, Libertarians believe in severely limiting the functions of the federal government. Their plan would: cut the budget by two-thirds; end all government programs except the military, police, and prisons; open all borders; and abolish the income tax. Since 1972, they have backed political candidates at all levels of government, even the presidency.

But tax protesters reside at the other end of the political spectrum as well. Some refuse to pay their taxes because they feel too much of their money goes for military spending. The earliest protests came from religious groups, such as Quakers or Mennonites. One of the most famous resisters is the writer Henry David Thoreau (1817–1862). He went to jail in 1846 because he refused to pay a poll tax that raised money for the Mexican-American War. Thoreau went on to write "Civil Disobedience" and *Walden*.

Each time the country increases its spending on the military, the number of pacifist (people against the use of force) tax resisters increase. In the mid-1980s military spending rose dramatically. The National War Tax Resistance Coordinating Committee estimated that between ten thousand and twenty thousand Americans refused to pay part or all of their income tax.

The Effects of the Sixteenth Amendment

The Sixteenth Amendment was the final result of a long process involving generations of American lawmakers who worked to create effective forms of taxation. It has had far-reaching effects.

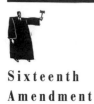

Sixteenth Amendment

It gave the federal government a consistent source of revenue—something all governments need in order to pay their operating expenses. But this burden of paying taxes is a fair one, and is divided between the people so that everyone pays a reasonable amount based on what they earn. Income tax also gives citizens a personal reason to participate in their national government, because the money Congress spends comes directly from the people. Citizens are more actively concerned about government spending, and tax laws. They pay more attention to what their elected representatives do about these things, and express their opinions by voting for candidates that they believe will use their money wisely.

From Salmon Chase's first income tax proposal in 1862 to President Woodrow Wilson's signing of the Sixteenth Amendment in 1913, income tax was meant to be positive and to make taxation as fair as possible. Future generations of taxpayers will continue to make changes in the tax code as they continue trying to balance the people's happiness and success with the public good.

For More Information

Books

Adams, Charles. *Those Dirty Rotten Taxes: The Tax Revolts That Built America.* New York: Free Press, 1998.

Bernstein, Richard B., with Jerome Agel. *Amending America: If We Love the Constitution So Much, Why Do We Keep Trying to Change It?* New York: Times Books/Random House, 1993; Lawrence, KS: University Press of Kansas, 1995.

Bradford, David F. *Untangling the Income Tax.* Lincoln, NE: iUniverse.com, 1986.

Burnham, David. *A Law Unto Itself: Power, Politics and the IRS.* New York: Random House, 1990.

Carson, Gerald. *The Golden Egg: The Personal Income Tax: Where It Came from, How It Grew.* New York: Houghton Mifflin Company, 1977.

Carson, Gerald. "Income Tax." *The Reader's Companion to American History, Edition 1991.* Edited by Eric Foner and John A Garrity. New York: Houghton and Mifflin, 1991.

Larson, Martin A. *The Continuing Tax Rebellion.* Old Greenwich, CT: Devin-Adair Publishers, 1979.

Levi, Margaret. *Of Rule and Revenue.* Berkeley, CA: University of California Press, 1988.

Morin, Isobel V. *Our Changing Constitution: How and Why We Have Amended It.* Brookfield, CT: Millbrook Press, 1998.

Pechman, Joseph A. *The Rich, the Poor, and the Taxes They Pay.* Boulder, CO: Westview Press, 1986.

Ratner, Sidney. *Taxation and Democracy in America.* New York: Octagon Books, 1970.

Reese, Thomas J. *The Politics of Taxation.* Westport, CT: Quorum Books, 1980.

Seligman, Edwin Robert Anderson. *The Income Tax: A Study of the History, Theory, and Practice of Income Taxation at Home and Abroad.* New York: Macmillan, 1914.

Stern, Philip M. *The Great Treasury Raid.* New York: Random House, 1964.

Zinn, Howard. *A People's History of the United States.* New York: Harper and Row, 1980.

Articles

Birnbaum Jeffrey H. "A Tax Protest That Doth Protest Too Much, Wethinks." *Fortune* 139, no.10 (1999 May 24): 326.

Caplan, Richard. "People Who Are Deducting Defense: The War-Tax Resisters." *The Nation* 240 (1985 April 6): 399–401.

"The Far, Far Right." *Canada and the World Backgrounder* 62, no.1 (September 1996): 26–29.

"Just What Do They Mean When They Talk Taxes" (Do the Rich Really Pay More?) *Congressional Quarterly Weekly Report* 48, no. 24 (1990 June 16): 1857–63.

Rust, Michael, and Susan Crabtree. "Libertarians Crash the Gates of Big Government." *Insight on the News* 12, no. 28, (1996 July 29): 15–17.

Saunders, Laura. "Original Sins: U.S. Tax System." *Forbes* 140 (1987 July 13): 286–89.

**Sixteenth
Amendment**

Web sites

Koeller, David W. "North Park UniversityHistory DepartmentWebChron."
    [Online] http://www.npcts.edu/acad/history/WebChron/USA/
    Progressive (accessed on 20 June, 2000).

Seventeenth Amendment

The Senate of the United States shall be composed of two Senators from each State, elected by the people thereof, for six years; and each Senator shall have one vote. The electors in each State shall have the qualifications requisite for electors of the most numerous branch of the State legislatures.

When vacancies happen in the representation of any State in the Senate, the executive authority of such State shall issue writs of election to fill such vacancies: *Provided*, That the legislature of any State may empower the executive thereof to make temporary appointments until the people fill the vacancies by election as the legislature may direct.

This amendment shall not be so construed as to affect the election or term of any Senator chosen before it becomes valid as part of the Constitution.

The Seventeenth Amendment is the only constitutional amendment to change the fundamental structure of the government as originally drafted in the Constitution. The Seventeenth Amendment increased the American public's ability to control the federal government, because it granted voters the opportunity to directly elect their representatives to the Senate. Before the amendment was ratified in 1913, state legislatures chose Senators.

When the Constitution was written in 1787, many citizens wanted a "loose" union between the former colonies. This left the states with considerable powers to rule themselves as they wished. Under the original terms of the Constitution, the congressional houses divided the government's power between the people and the states. Members popularly elected to the House of Representatives represented the American people, and states chose Senators to represent them. The

RATIFICATION FACTS

PROPOSED: Submitted by Congress to the states on May 13, 1912.

RATIFICATION: Ratified by the required three-fourths of states (thirty-six of forty-eight) by April 8, 1913, and by nine more states by March 9, 1922. Declared to be part of the Constitution on May 31, 1913.

RATIFYING STATES: Massachusetts, May 22, 1912; Arizona, June 3, 1912; Minnesota, June 10, 1912; New York, January 15, 1913; Kansas, January 17, 1913; Oregon, January 23, 1913; North Carolina, January 25, 1913; California, January 28, 1913; Michigan, January 28, 1913; Iowa, January 30, 1913; Montana, January 30, 1913; Idaho, January 31, 1913; West Virginia, February 4, 1913; Colorado, February 5, 1913; Nevada, February 6, 1913; Texas, February 7, 1913; Washington, February 7, 1913; Wyoming, February 8, 1913; Arkansas, February 11, 1913; Maine, February 11, 1913; Illinois, February 13, 1913; North Dakota, February 14, 1913; Wisconsin, February 18, 1913; Indiana, February 19, 1913; New Hampshire, February 19, 1913; Vermont, February 19, 1913; South Dakota, February 19, 1913; Oklahoma, February 24, 1913; Ohio, February 25, 1913; Missouri, March 7, 1913; New Mexico, March 13, 1913; Nebraska, March 14, 1913; New Jersey, March 17, 1913; Tennessee, April 1, 1913; Pennsylvania, April 2, 1913; Connecticut, April 8, 1913.

Seventeenth Amendment shifted the division of power in the government, and gave the American people direct control over who represented their state in both the House of Representatives and the Senate.

Origins of the Seventeenth Amendment

When statesmen congregated (gathered) at Independence Hall in Philadelphia in 1787, they intended to alter the Articles of Confederation, and provide the framework for the new nation's government. The Articles of Confederation outlined a country united by a weak federal government and strong states. The statesmen soon realized that a much stronger central government was needed in order to keep the union stable and at peace. They defined this new government in the Constitution.

Checks and balances

Having just won freedom from the unresponsive British monarchy, the American statesmen worked to create a responsive government of and by the people. Some statesmen feared that giving the public too much authority would subject the government to popular whims, and lead to chaos and instability. These statesmen favored a government that included a system of checks and balances between the governing bodies.

The checks and balances would protect the American people from themselves by allowing separate parts of the government to deliberate (talk) on an issue before committing the country to action. The resulting Constitution detailed such a system of checks and balances. In letters known as the *Federalist,* Alexander Hamilton (1755–1804), James Madison (1751–1836; president 1809–17), and John Jay (1745–1829) wrote that the checks and balances would protect the government and American people from "the blow meditated by the people against themselves, until reason, justice, and truth can regain their authority over the public mind."

PROTECTING THE PEOPLE FROM THEMSELVES. The Senate's primary role in the new government was to provide a check on all legislation passed by Congress, or the lower house. It would also reject any treaty or political appointment initiated by the president. The framers of the Constitution reasoned that citizens were qualified to make good decisions about their representatives in the state legislatures. However, the framers felt those same citizens would not make good choices of senators to represent their state in the federal government.

The framers feared that citizens might vote for undeserving politicians, or that corrupt political interest groups who would take "advantage of the [indifference], the ignorance, and the hopes and fears of the unwary and interested." The framers of the Constitution considered the Senate an anchor against such corruption.

In addition, the framers considered a Senate chosen by state legislatures a good balance against a popularly elected Congress. The framers thought it unlikely that special interest groups would gain control if both houses were elected by different means. This would let the Senate and the Congress form a barrier against an interest group gaining control of legislative power. During the deliberations in Independence Hall, only James Wilson of Pennsylvania argued for the direct election (election by the people) of senators. But the decision to let state legislatures vote for senators was eventually adopted unanimously.

THE GREAT COMPROMISE. The number of senators serving in the Senate was determined during the Federal Convention of 1787 in what is known as the Great Compromise. Individual states differed in size. They argued about how to select government representatives: depending on the state's population, or regardless of size. They compromised, and created the House of Representatives. The House would represent the people of the states, and the Senate would represent the individual states. Two senators would represent each state. Large and small states alike were satisfied with the arrangement, and never again competed for more representation at the federal level.

Corruption in the Senate

Until the end of the Civil War (1861–1865), the U.S. Senate enjoyed a reputation as the "greatest deliberative (thinking) body in the Western world." The Senate garnered the attention and praise of influential foreign dignitaries. After the Civil War, however, the Senate turned into a place where the interests of big businesses soon carried more weight than reasoned debate.

After the Civil War, great wealth was generated for a small group of businessmen as industries consolidated (combined) and started to serve national markets. Railroads and other transportation companies were among those corporations that grew to serve a national market. Never before had so few companies controlled so much economic power. For example, the areas where railroads laid their tracks enjoyed more jobs, more tourists, and more access to markets than other areas.

Big business takes over

State legislatures quickly learned that they could use senatorial seats to gain favor with the influential businesses that brought wealth and jobs to their states. In turn, businessmen pursued senatorial seats when federal regulations started to impose limits on, or to provide benefits to, their businesses. In large cities like Chicago, Illinois, Kansas City, Missouri, and New York, New York, political bosses (businessmen who exerted a controlling force on political decisions) soon gained enough power to influence senatorial elections.

Political bosses and other influential politicians and businessmen bought the votes of state legislatures, or strong-armed (bullied) them, to effectively control who became a United States Senator. If a candidate was not favored, wealthy businessmen or lobbyists for certain industries gave huge sums of money to all candidates. The money did not support a certain political viewpoint. Instead, the winning candidate was obligated to whoever gave him the money.

Senator Chauncey Mitchell Depew (1834–1928) was a prime example of this corruption. David Graham Phillips (see sidebar), muckraker (a person who seeks and exposes misconduxt in public life) wrote an article about Depew. He called Senator Depew "an ideal lieutenant for a plutocrat," and exposed Senator Depew's connection with furthering the interests of the powerful William H. Vanderbilt family. (The Vanderbilt's tried to push through legislation that would benefit their railroad between New York City and Buffalo, New York.) Phillips also linked corrupt senators and businessmen to legislation concerning beef inspection, food and drug purity standards, railroad regulations, and sugar subsidies (government granted money) among other things.

Muckrakers expose big business

The American public was not blind to the Senate's corruption. Muckraking articles appeared in magazines and newspapers, and told the tales of the corruption. The stories of the purchase of senatorial votes by political interest groups or wealthy businessmen were fantastic and sometimes exaggerated. However, they generated intense scrutiny of the Senate, and the voting records of its members. Skeptical people rejected the notion that many senators could be bribed, but they were also not blind to the number of millionaires in the Senate.

THE MILLIONAIRE'S CLUB. The Senate became known as The Millionaire's Club, The Rich Man's Club, and the House of Dollars. Among the millionaire senators were: Philetus Sawyer of Wisconsin, who made his millions in lumber; California railroad magnate Leland Stanford; Arthur Gorman of Maryland, who ran the Chesapeake and Ohio Canal Company; and Nelson Aldrich of Rhode Island, who made millions in banking. The opinion that the Senate represented corporate wealth grew in popularity.

STATE LEGISLATURES HINDER SENATORIAL ELECTIONS. Corporate influence in the Senate was not the only problem with the legislative body. In the early 1800s, some states provided senators with written instructions for how they should vote on certain issues. Some senators resigned when their own beliefs did not coincide with their state's wishes. Among them were John Quincy Adams (1767–1848; president 1825–29) in 1807, and John Tyler (1790–1862; president 1841–45) of Virginia in 1836. By the mid-

1800s, states stopped making rules for how senators voted.

THE INFLUENCE OF POLITICAL PARTIES IN SENATORIAL ELECTIONS. Some historians trace the influence of political parties in senatorial elections back to the first one in 1789. Early political parties represented different factions or commercial interests within the state. By the mid-1800s, political parties were more nationally organized, and dominated senatorial elections.

In some states, political parties would hold state conventions to choose their party's nominee. The party's representatives in the state legislature then promised to vote for their party's nominee. Sometimes politicians were unwilling to vote for someone of another political party,

John Tyler resigned his senatorial position when he found that his own beliefs did not coincide with the wishes of the state he was representing. He went on to become the tenth president of the United States. Courtesy of the Library of Congress.

and debates in state legislatures dragged on for months. Occasionally, this left states without representatives during some Congresses.

DEADLOCK. George H. Haynes, a respected Senate historian, wrote that the sessions would sometimes degenerate into "riotous demonstrations more appropriate to a prize-fight than to a senatorial election." In one particularly colorful instance, the Missouri state legislators threw fists, desks, and books at each other. The fight erupted over whether to break the wall clock, and allow deliberations over senatorial selections to continue after the scheduled hour of adjournment (closing). One member finally broke the clock by hurling ink bottles at it. "It is ridiculous to suggest that amid scenes like these the choice of a senator retains anything of the character of an exercise of cool judgment."

These types of sessions resulted in poor decisions, or no decisions at all. The most extreme case of state legislature paralysis was in Delaware. The Delaware state legislature's inability to elect even one senator left the state without any representation in the federal government between 1901 and 1903. Other states succeeded in electing only one senator, or elected senators after the Senate had already started a session.

A Push for Direct Election of Senators

Between 1826 and 1912, more than 197 resolutions for direct election of senators were introduced in the House of Representatives. Only six received the necessary two-thirds majority vote needed to reach the Senate. Once in the Senate, all such resolutions were ignored. In 1910, the only resolution ever debated lost by a narrow margin.

As the Senate continued to ignore the public's will over the years, reformers of the election process were forced to unite across political parties. Though movement in the federal legislature was slow, political pressures to change the election process for senators gradually built momentum.

As early as the 1880s and 1890s, reform advocates (supporters) declared that "special interests had conspired to hold the Senate hostage," and "the documentation they presented to the public painted a horrifying picture of a widespread network of corrupt bargains, in which wealth and power were exchanged for influence and votes."

Political parties made direct election of senators part of their presidential platforms. It started with the Peoples Party between 1892 and 1904, and was followed by the Democratic Party in 1900 and 1904, and then the Prohibition Party in 1904. The Pennsylvania legislature proposed a second Constitutional Convention in 1900. By 1905, thirty-one states had either passed referendums proposing that Congress consider a constitutional amendment, or otherwise voiced their support for direct election.

With the publication of muckraking articles like David Graham Phillips's "The Treason of the Senate" that appeared in *Cosmopolitan Magazine* in 1906, public interest in direct election mounted. Demand for reform was so great that the fifty-seventh Congress printed an additional five thousand copies of the Senate committee report on direct election.

MUCKRAKING AND THE
SEVENTEENTH AMENDMENT

Muckraking is a form of journalism. It was used in the early 1900s, and boldly attempted to reveal some essential truth about public figures, political issues, or institutions. Muckrakers published articles that exposed corruptions in American government. According to George E. Mowry and Judson A. Grenier, muckrakers followed the advice of a biblical passage from St. John: "And ye shall know the truth and the truth shall make you free."

The articles enjoyed a great deal of popularity. Journalists such as Samuel Hopkins Adams, Ray Stannard Baker, Charles Edward Russell, Upton Sinclair, and Ida M. Tarbell became household names. Their vivid articles reached the readers of magazines like *McClure's, Collier's,* the *American,* and the *Cosmopolitan.*

Muckrakers were primarily concerned with exposing the privileges that money bought in political life. The industrial revolution had created great wealth, but only for a very few. Muckrakers worked hard to show just how much influence this new wealth affected the government.

The villains in the thousands of muckraking stories were greedy businessmen, or what muckrakers called "predatory wealth." To stop these corrupt businessmen, muckrakers called for greater democracy. They considered it "the inevitable sequence of widespread intelli-

A report of the Senate conducted during the fifty-eighth Congress (1903–1905) was published in 1906. It revealed that "[O]ne senator out of every three owes his election to his personal wealth, to his being the candidate satisfactory to what is coming to be called the 'System,' or to his expertness in political manipulation—qualifications which make their usefulness as members of the dominant branch of Congress decidedly open to question."

In 1906 alone, nine resolutions for direct election were put before Congress. The American public agreed that direct election would free the Senate from corrupting influences. In 1911, Indiana representative John A. Adair argued in Congress that direct election would fill the Senate

gence." Publishers also made greater democracy a rallying cry. As early as February 5, 1899, William Randolph Hearst's newspapers made the direct election of United States Senators a firm editorial quest.

The height of the Muckraking Era came in 1906 when David Graham Phillips published "The Treason of the Senate" articles in *Cosmopolitan Magazine.* In his articles, Phillips examined the corruption of the Senate. One of the most important issues Phillips tackled was the millionaires in the Senate.

Charles Edward Russell was a fellow muckraker who believed the Senate was made up of senators who used their seats to make millions, Russell called the Senate a house made up of "butlers for industrialists and financiers."

Phillips reported that as many as twenty-five senators were millionaires at the time of his writing. (Some scholars estimate the number was actually closer to ten.) Powerful businessmen with great interest in creating laws to protect their companies often sought election. Phillips wondered whether it was better to elect these millionaires, or to have them bribe senators.

Phillips profiled the careers of twenty-one senators, and declared that senatorial selection was based on private wealth and power in party organizations. Phillips called senators "grafters," "bribers," and "perjurers," and exposed decisions where senators favored the interests of their corporate backers over the interests of the public. *(continued on page 346)*

with people with "rugged honesty, recognized ability, admitted capacity, and wide experience."

Popular election of senators without an amendment

Reformers looked for alternatives when they were unable to pass amendment proposals through the Senate, or to gain enough support for a second Constitutional Convention. To appease popular pressure for direct election of senators, some states invented a new voting method to allow the public to select senators. The new method was called a primary election.

Oregon developed the first primary elections between 1901 and 1904. With this method, people voted for candidates in primary elections.

MUCKRAKING AND THE SEVENTEENTH AMENDMENT *(Continued)*

President Theodore Roosevelt (1858–1919; president 1901–09)grew more frustrated with each monthly muckraking installment. He told the *Post* editor that

"Phillips takes certain facts that are true in themselves, and by ignoring utterly a very much larger mass of facts that are just as true and just as important, and by down-right perversion of truth both in the way of misstatement and of omission, succeeds in giving a totally false picture... [The articles] give no accurate guide for those who are really anxious to war against corruption, and they do excite a hysterical and ignorant feeling against everything existing, good or bad ..."

But Phillips responded to critics by stating that "these articles have been attacked, but their facts—the facts of the treason of the Senate, taken from the records—have not been attacked. Abuse is not refutation (wrong); it is confession." He added, "The exposed cry out that these exposures endanger the Republic. What a ludicrous inversion—the burglar shouting that the house is falling because he is being ejected from it? The Republic is not in danger; it is its enemies that are in danger."

In the end, *The Treason of the Senate* and other muckraking articles stirred what President Roosevelt labeled "a revolutionary feeling in the country." The muckraking articles were read by hundreds of thousands of people, and helped reformers generate popular consensus for the eventual ratification of the Seventeenth Amendment.

The state legislatures would then officially elect the primary's winner to the senate. Candidates pledged to uphold the popular primary elections during their tenure. Primary elections quickly delivered the desired reduction in deadlock and corruption in senatorial elections. An Oregon paper reported in 1907 that "On the first ballot, in twenty minutes, we elected two Senators, without boodle, or booze, or even a cigar!" By 1910, fourteen of the thirty states used primary elections to select senators.

Race and Ratification

There was another issue that complicated the political power struggle over senatorial elections between the American public and the corporate interests: the power of black votes. Black votes could influence senatorial elections, and this was why some southern senators were reluctant about direct election proposals.

The South had a long history of denying blacks the right to vote. The Fourteenth Amendment established equal rights for all citizens. The Fifteenth Amendment granted people of all races and colors the right to vote. Even after these amendments were ratified, southern states implemented poll taxes and literacy tests to keep as many blacks as possible from voting. To ensure that whites retained control at the polls, southern Democrats insisted that every proposal for direct election gave states the authority to regulate elections.

The race rider

A proposal for the first vote on direct election in the full Senate emerged from the Senate's Judiciary Committee in 1910. The proposal had a provision that proved so controversial it doomed the proposal from a passing vote. The provision was nicknamed the "race rider."

The race rider ensured that states would control election regulations. It had been added in the Judiciary Committee as a compromise to win Democratic votes. But when senators in the full Senate debated the proposal, many balked at the race rider. They declared it would effectively reverse the Fifteenth Amendment by allowing states to racially discriminate against some voters. Chauncey Depew of New York opposed it, saying that passing the proposal would be "deliberately voting to undo the results of the Civil War."

The direct election amendment failed to pass in the Senate in 1910, but several senators encouraged continued discussion of the issue. Over the next year, the House and the Senate continued to debate the race rider. The rider was the only real obstacle to the direct election proposal passing in both houses. After two months of intense debate, the Senate almost passed the proposal without the race rider on February 28, 1911. It was a fifty-four to thirty-three margin (four not voting)—just four votes short of the needed two-thirds majority.

Congress went back and forth over the addition or removal of the race rider. The House voted on the amendment issue again in April, 1911.

**Seventeenth
Amendment**

The amendment passed with a race rider by a margin of 296 to 16 (70 not voting). The Senate discarded the race rider, and passed the revised proposal with the required two-thirds supermajority by a margin of 64 to 24 (three not voting). Instead of quickly passing the revised version of the proposal, the House entered into yet further debate. Representative Walter Rucker proposed to abandon the race rider on May 13, 1912. The House voted again, and this time passed the revised amendment proposal by a margin of 238 to 39 (five voted "present," and 110 not voting).

Unlike the congressional houses, the states did not wrangle over the direct-election amendment. The amendment swiftly passed through state legislatures in less than a year, and became the Seventeenth Amendment on April 8, 1913. Although the amendment decreased the power of the states, the state legislatures seemed more than happy to pass it. With the use of primary elections, many of the U.S. Senators had already been selected by popular vote. To many, the ratification of the Seventeenth Amendment simply formalized a practice of direct election that was already widely used.

The Progressive Amendments

The Seventeenth Amendment is tied to a time between when Americans united, and gave themselves more control over their public and private lives. The time is called the Progressive Era, and it lasted from about 1900 to 1920. The "Progressive" amendments are: the Sixteenth Amendment, the Seventeenth Amendment, and the Nineteenth Amendment. (The Sixteenth Amendment established a federal income tax, and the Nineteenth Amendment gave women the right to vote.)

The Seventeenth Amendment made the federal government more democratic. It was the greatest alteration to the workings of the state and federal governments since the Civil War Amendments—the Thirteenth, Fourteenth, and Fifteenth Amendments. (Together, they abolished slavery, established equal rights for all citizens, and granted people of all races and colors the right to vote.)

New ways to use amendments

The passage of the Sixteenth and the Seventeenth Amendments in 1913 ushered in a wave of new thinking about the purpose of constitutional amendments. During the forty years following the Civil War, no constitutional amendments were ratified. Hundreds of amendments were proposed during those forty years. The problem was, none could gain the two-thirds majority vote needed to ratify them. Politicians and social advocates questioned the usefulness of the Constitution, thinking it seemed rather inflexible.

But when two constitutional amendments were ratified in the same year, constitutional amendments seemed like realistic solutions to a variety of social and political problems. The American public recognized the power constitutional amendments had to redirect the activities of government. Perhaps more importantly, Americans also realized their own ability to effectively change the Constitution to create a government that was responsive to their needs and desires.

The ratification of the Sixteenth and Seventeenth Amendments in the same year was "a political reaction to the great concentration of wealth and its alleged corrupting influence on the political system." In reaction to the alterations in the country's economic structure brought about by the Civil War, the American public demanded a more equal tax structure. The Sixteenth Amendment provided that tax structure, and laid the ground work for diluting (weakening) the concentration of wealth in the country.

But the public grew frustrated as it heard about the Senate debates over the Sixteenth Amendment. Senators who owned or were influenced by the large corporations tried to block the amendment. This drew the public's attention to the great number of millionaires in the Senate. The public was angry that the wealthy senators would not pass a more equitable tax system, and they wondered how to make the senators more responsive to their desires. Public outcry to the senators' attempts to block the Sixteenth Amendment helped to push the Seventeenth Amendment through the Senate.

The Sixteenth and Seventeenth Amendment paved the way for Progressive advocates to succeed in passing the other Progressive amendments. The other amendments were designed to take control of government from large corporations and give it back to the people. Constitutional amendments fixed more than just governmental procedural problems. They were ways to restrict alcohol use, grant voting rights for women, and regulate child labor.

Effects of the Seventeenth Amendment

The Seventeenth Amendment succeeded in some ways, but failed in others. The Seventeenth Amendment has made the Senate more responsive to

**Seventeenth
Amendment**

the American public. The American public has greater access to senators, and can influence senators' decisions on many issues of national and international importance. Senators, who must run for election and reelection, try to maintain an openness and responsiveness to public opinion.

One area in which the Senate has been accused of being too responsive to the public is in its handling of presidential appointments to the Supreme Court. Public opinion heavily influenced Senate reactions during two appointment processes. One in 1987 when President Ronald Reagan nominated Judge Robert H. Bork, and again in 1991 when President George Bush successfully appointed Clarence Thomas to the Supreme Court.

The Senate has been accused of taking public opinion too much into consideration in instance such as the nomination of Judge Robert H. Bork to the Supreme Court in 1987. Reproduced by permission of Corbis-Bettmann.

The Senate's Judiciary Committee considers Supreme Court candidates, and can also generate public reaction. News stories triggered strong public opposition to the Bork and Thomas nominations. The news reported about Judge Bork's controversial opinions, and there were televised hearings of sexual harassment charges brought by a former employee against Judge Thomas.

Although many anticipated that direct election would make U.S. Senators prone to popular whims, the Seventeenth Amendment also changed the Senate in unexpected ways. Rather than ridding the Senate of millionaires, the amendment has heightened the importance of money in the Senate.

Compared to the ten millionaires in the senate at the turn of the century, there were more than twenty-five by the mid-1990s. Senators must constantly campaign in order to raise the funds needed for reelection. It is estimated that senators must raise approximately $15 thousand for each week of their six-year terms. Candidates in California have spent more than $10 million to secure a senate seat. By the 1990s, an average expenditure per seat in other states reached $5 million.

Seventeenth
Amendment

For More Information

Books

Bernstein, Richard B., with Jerome Agel. *Amending America: If We Love the Constitution So Much, Why Do We Keep Trying to Change It?* New York: Times Books, 1993.

Feinberg, Barbara Silberdick. *Constitutional Amendments.* New York: Twenty-First Century Books, 1996.

Grimes, Alan P. *Democracy and the Amendments to the Constitution.* Lexington, KY: D. C. Heath and Company, 1978.

Hamilton, Alexander, Jay, John, and James Madison. *The Federalist.* New York: Modern Library, 1937.

Haynes, George H. *The Senate of the United States: Its History and Practice.* 2 vols. Boston: Houghton Mifflin Co., 1938.

Hoebeke, C. H. *The Road to Mass Democracy: Original Intent and the Seventeenth Amendment.* New Brunswick, NJ: Transaction, 1995.

Kyvig, David E. *Explicit and Authentic Acts: Amending the U.S. Constitution, 1776–1995.* Lawrence, KS: University of Press of Kansas, 1996.

Mabie, Margot C. J. *The Constitution: Reflections of a Changing Nation.* New York: Henry Holt Books, 1987.

Palmer, Kris E., ed. *Constitutional Amendments, 1789 to the Present.* Detroit: Gale Group, 2000.

Phillips, David Graham. *The Treason of the Senate.* Edited with an introduction by George E. Mowry and Judson A. Grenier. Chicago: Quadrangle Books, 1964.

Sectionhead

Web sites

The Center for Constitutional Studies. [Online] http://www.nhumanities.
    org/ccs-res.htm (accessed August 2000).

The U.S. Constitution Online. [Online] http:/www.usconstitution.net/
    constnot.html (accessed August 2000).

Constitution of the United States of America

We the People of the United States, in Order to form a more perfect Union, establish Justice, insure domestic Tranquility, provide for the common defense, promote the general Welfare, and secure the Blessings of Liberty to ourselves and our Posterity, do ordain and establish this Constitution for the United States of America.

Article I

Items in italic have since been amended or superseded.
A portion of Article I, Section 2, was modified by Section 2 of the Fourteenth Amendment; Article I, Section 3, was modified by the Seventeenth Amendment; Article I, Section 4, was modified by Section 2 of the Twentieth Amendment; and Article I, Section 9, was modified by the Sixteenth Amendment.

Section 1.

All legislative Powers herein granted shall be vested in a Congress of the United States, which shall consist of a Senate and House of Representatives.

Section 2.

The House of Representatives shall be composed of Members chosen every second Year by the People of the several States, and the Electors in each State shall have the Qualifications requisite for Electors of the most numerous Branch of the State Legislature.

No Person shall be a Representative who shall not have attained to the Age of twenty five Years, and been seven Years a Citizen of the

United States, and who shall not, when elected, be an Inhabitant of that State in which he shall be chosen.

Representatives and direct Taxes shall be apportioned among the several States which may be included within this Union, according to their respective Numbers, which shall be determined by adding to the whole Number of free Persons, including those bound to Service for a Term of Years, and excluding Indians not taxed, three fifths of all other Persons. The actual Enumeration shall be made within three Years after the first Meeting of the Congress of the United States, and within every subsequent Term of ten Years, in such Manner as they shall by Law direct. The Number of Representatives shall not exceed one for every thirty Thousand, but each State shall have at Least one Representative; and until such enumeration shall be made, the State of New Hampshire shall be entitled to chuse three, Massachusetts eight, Rhode-Island and Providence Plantations one, Connecticut five, New-York six, New Jersey four, Pennsylvania eight, Delaware one, Maryland six, Virginia ten, North Carolina five, South Carolina five, and Georgia three.

When vacancies happen in the Representation from any State, the Executive Authority thereof shall issue Writs of Election to fill such Vacancies.

The House of Representatives shall chuse their Speaker and other Officers; and shall have the sole Power of Impeachment.

Section 3.

The Senate of the United States shall be composed of two Senators from each State, *chosen by the Legislature thereof* for six Years; and each Senator shall have one Vote.

Immediately after they shall be assembled in Consequence of the first Election, they shall be divided as equally as may be into three Classes. The Seats of the Senators of the first Class shall be vacated at the Expiration of the second Year, of the second Class at the Expiration of the fourth Year, and of the third Class at the Expiration of the sixth Year, so that one third may be chosen every second Year; *and if Vacancies happen by Resignation, or otherwise, during the Recess of the Legislature of any State, the Executive thereof may make temporary Appointments until the next Meeting of the Legislature, which shall then fill such Vacancies.*

No Person shall be a Senator who shall not have attained to the Age of thirty Years, and been nine Years a Citizen of the United States, and who shall not, when elected, be an Inhabitant of that State for which he shall be chosen.

The Vice President of the United States shall be President of the Senate, but shall have no Vote, unless they be equally divided.

The Senate shall chuse their other Officers, and also a President pro tempore, in the Absence of the Vice President, or when he shall exercise the Office of President of the United States.

The Senate shall have the sole Power to try all Impeachments. When sitting for that Purpose, they shall be on Oath or Affirmation. When the President of the United States is tried, the Chief Justice shall preside: And no Person shall be convicted without the Concurrence of two thirds of the Members present.

Judgment in Cases of Impeachment shall not extend further than to removal from Office, and disqualification to hold and enjoy any Office of honor, Trust or Profit under the United States: but the Party convicted shall nevertheless be liable and subject to Indictment, Trial, Judgment and Punishment, according to Law.

Section 4.

The Times, Places and Manner of holding Elections for Senators and Representatives, shall be prescribed in each State by the Legislature thereof; but the Congress may at any time by Law make or alter such Regulations, except as to the Places of chusing Senators.

The Congress shall assemble at least once in every Year, and such Meeting shall *be on the first Monday in December,* unless they shall by Law appoint a different Day.

Section 5.

Each House shall be the Judge of the Elections, Returns and Qualifications of its own Members, and a Majority of each shall constitute a Quorum to do Business; but a smaller Number may adjourn from day to day, and may be authorized to compel the Attendance of absent Members, in such Manner, and under such Penalties as each House may provide.

Each House may determine the Rules of its Proceedings, punish its Members for disorderly Behaviour, and, with the Concurrence of two thirds, expel a Member.

Each House shall keep a Journal of its Proceedings, and from time to time publish the same, excepting such Parts as may in their Judgment

Constitution
of the United
States of
America

require Secrecy; and the Yeas and Nays of the Members of either House on any question shall, at the Desire of one fifth of those Present, be entered on the Journal.

Neither House, during the Session of Congress, shall, without the Consent of the other, adjourn for more than three days, nor to any other Place than that in which the two Houses shall be sitting.

Section 6.

The Senators and Representatives shall receive a Compensation for their Services, to be ascertained by Law, and paid out of the Treasury of the United States. They shall in all Cases, except Treason, Felony and Breach of the Peace, be privileged from Arrest during their Attendance at the Session of their respective Houses, and in going to and returning from the same; and for any Speech or Debate in either House, they shall not be questioned in any other Place.

No Senator or Representative shall, during the Time for which he was elected, be appointed to any civil Office under the Authority of the United States, which shall have been created, or the Emoluments where-of shall have been encreased during such time; and no Person holding any Office under the United States, shall be a Member of either House during his Continuance in Office.

Section 7.

All Bills for raising Revenue shall originate in the House of Representatives; but the Senate may propose or concur with Amendments as on other Bills.

Every Bill which shall have passed the House of Representatives and the Senate, shall, before it become a Law, be presented to the President of the United States: If he approve he shall sign it, but if not he shall return it, with his Objections to that House in which it shall have originated, who shall enter the Objections at large on their Journal, and proceed to reconsider it. If after such Reconsideration two thirds of that House shall agree to pass the Bill, it shall be sent, together with the Objections, to the other House, by which it shall likewise be reconsid-ered, and if approved by two thirds of that House, it shall become a Law. But in all such Cases the Votes of both Houses shall be determined by yeas and Nays, and the Names of the Persons voting for and against the Bill shall be entered on the Journal of each House respectively. If any Bill shall not be returned by the President within ten Days (Sundays excepted) after it shall have been presented to him, the Same shall be a Law, in like Manner as if he had signed it, unless the Congress by their Adjournment prevent its Return, in which Case it shall not be a Law.

Every Order, Resolution, or Vote to which the Concurrence of the Senate and House of Representatives may be necessary (except on a question of Adjournment) shall be presented to the President of the United States; and before the Same shall take Effect, shall be approved by him, or being disapproved by him, shall be repassed by two thirds of the Senate and House of Representatives, according to the Rules and Limitations prescribed in the Case of a Bill.

Section 8.

The Congress shall have Power To lay and collect Taxes, Duties, Imposts and Excises, to pay the Debts and provide for the common Defence and general Welfare of the United States; but all Duties, Imposts and Excises shall be uniform throughout the United States;

To borrow Money on the credit of the United States;

To regulate Commerce with foreign Nations, and among the several States, and with the Indian Tribes;

To establish an uniform Rule of Naturalization, and uniform Laws on the subject of Bankruptcies throughout the United States;

To coin Money, regulate the Value thereof, and of foreign Coin, and fix the Standard of Weights and Measures;

To provide for the Punishment of counterfeiting the Securities and current Coin of the United States;

To establish Post Offices and post Roads;

To promote the Progress of Science and useful Arts, by securing for limited Times to Authors and Inventors the exclusive Right to their respective Writings and Discoveries;

To constitute Tribunals inferior to the supreme Court;

To define and punish Piracies and Felonies committed on the high Seas, and Offences against the Law of Nations;

To declare War, grant Letters of Marque and Reprisal, and make Rules concerning Captures on Land and Water;

To raise and support Armies, but no Appropriation of Money to that Use shall be for a longer Term than two Years;

To provide and maintain a Navy;

To make Rules for the Government and Regulation of the land and naval Forces;

To provide for calling forth the Militia to execute the Laws of the Union, suppress Insurrections and repel Invasions;

To provide for organizing, arming, and disciplining, the Militia, and for governing such Part of them as may be employed in the Service of the United States, reserving to the States respectively, the Appointment of the Officers, and the Authority of training the Militia according to the discipline prescribed by Congress;

To exercise exclusive Legislation in all Cases whatsoever, over such District (not exceeding ten Miles square) as may, by Cession of particular States, and the Acceptance of Congress, become the Seat of the Government of the United States, and to exercise like Authority over all Places purchased by the Consent of the Legislature of the State in which the Same shall be, for the Erection of Forts, Magazines, Arsenals, dock-Yards, and other needful Buildings;—And

To make all Laws which shall be necessary and proper for carrying into Execution the foregoing Powers, and all other Powers vested by this Constitution in the Government of the United States, or in any Department or Officer thereof.

Section 9.

The Migration or Importation of such Persons as any of the States now existing shall think proper to admit, shall not be prohibited by the Congress prior to the Year one thousand eight hundred and eight, but a Tax or duty may be imposed on such Importation, not exceeding ten dollars for each Person.

The Privilege of the Writ of Habeas Corpus shall not be suspended, unless when in Cases of Rebellion or Invasion the public Safety may require it.

No Bill of Attainder or ex post facto Law shall be passed.

No Capitation, or other direct, Tax shall be laid, *unless in Proportion to the Census or enumeration herein before directed to be taken.*

No Tax or Duty shall be laid on Articles exported from any State.

No Preference shall be given by any Regulation of Commerce or Revenue to the Ports of one State over those of another; nor shall

Vessels bound to, or from, one State, be obliged to enter, clear, or pay Duties in another.

No Money shall be drawn from the Treasury, but in Consequence of Appropriations made by Law; and a regular Statement and Account of the Receipts and Expenditures of all public Money shall be published from time to time.

No Title of Nobility shall be granted by the United States: And no Person holding any Office of Profit or Trust under them, shall, without the Consent of the Congress, accept of any present, Emolument, Office, or Title, of any kind whatever, from any King, Prince, or foreign State.

Section 10.

No State shall enter into any Treaty, Alliance, or Confederation; grant Letters of Marque and Reprisal; coin Money; emit Bills of Credit; make any Thing but gold and silver Coin a Tender in Payment of Debts; pass any Bill of Attainder, ex post facto Law, or Law impairing the Obligation of Contracts, or grant any Title of Nobility.

No State shall, without the Consent of the Congress, lay any Imposts or Duties on Imports or Exports, except what may be absolutely necessary for executing it's inspection Laws: and the net Produce of all Duties and Imposts, laid by any State on Imports or Exports, shall be for the Use of the Treasury of the United States; and all such Laws shall be subject to the Revision and Controul of the Congress.

No State shall, without the Consent of Congress, lay any Duty of Tonnage, keep Troops, or Ships of War in time of Peace, enter into any Agreement or Compact with another State, or with a foreign Power, or engage in War, unless actually invaded, or in such imminent Danger as will not admit of delay.

Article II

Article II, Section 1, was superseded by the Twelfth Amendment
Article II, Section 1, was modified by the Twenty-fifth Amendment.

Section 1.

The executive Power shall be vested in a President of the United States of America. He shall hold his Office during the Term of four Years, and, together with the Vice President, chosen for the same Term, be elected, as follows:

Each State shall appoint, in such Manner as the Legislature thereof may direct, a Number of Electors, equal to the whole Number of Senators and Representatives to which the State may be entitled in the Congress: but no Senator or Representative, or Person holding an Office of Trust or Profit under the United States, shall be appointed an Elector.

The Electors shall meet in their respective States, and vote by Ballot for two Persons, of whom one at least shall not be an Inhabitant of the same State with themselves. And they shall make a List of all the Persons voted for, and of the Number of Votes for each; which List they shall sign and certify, and transmit sealed to the Seat of the Government of the United States, directed to the President of the Senate. The President of the Senate shall, in the Presence of the Senate and House of Representatives, open all the Certificates, and the Votes shall then be counted. The Person having the greatest Number of Votes shall be the President, if such Number be a Majority of the whole Number of Electors appointed; and if there be more than one who have such Majority, and have an equal Number of Votes, then the House of Representatives shall immediately chuse by Ballot one of them for President; and if no Person have a Majority, then from the five highest on the List the said House shall in like Manner chuse the President. But in chusing the President, the Votes shall be taken by States, the Representation from each State having one Vote; A quorum for this purpose shall consist of a Member or Members from two thirds of the States, and a Majority of all the States shall be necessary to a Choice. In every Case, after the Choice of the President, the Person having the greatest Number of Votes of the Electors shall be the Vice President. But if there should remain two or more who have equal Votes, the Senate shall chuse from them by Ballot the Vice President.

The Congress may determine the Time of chusing the Electors, and the Day on which they shall give their Votes; which Day shall be the same throughout the United States.

No Person except a natural born Citizen, or a Citizen of the United States, at the time of the Adoption of this Constitution, shall be eligible to the Office of President; neither shall any Person be eligible to that Office who shall not have attained to the Age of thirty five Years, and been fourteen Years a Resident within the United States.

In Case of the Removal of the President from Office, or of his Death, Resignation, or Inability to discharge the Powers and Duties of the said Office, the Same shall devolve on the Vice President, and the Congress may by Law provide for the Case of Removal, Death, Resignation or

Inability, both of the President and Vice President, declaring what Officer shall then act as President, and such Officer shall act accordingly, until the Disability be removed, or a President shall be elected.

The President shall, at stated Times, receive for his Services, a Compensation, which shall neither be increased nor diminished during the Period for which he shall have been elected, and he shall not receive within that Period any other Emolument from the United States, or any of them.

Before he enter on the Execution of his Office, he shall take the following Oath or Affirmation:—"I do solemnly swear (or affirm) that I will faithfully execute the Office of President of the United States, and will to the best of my Ability, preserve, protect and defend the Constitution of the United States."

Section 2.

The President shall be Commander in Chief of the Army and Navy of the United States, and of the Militia of the several States, when called into the actual Service of the United States; he may require the Opinion, in writing, of the principal Officer in each of the executive Departments, upon any Subject relating to the Duties of their respective Offices, and he shall have Power to grant Reprieves and Pardons for Offences against the United States, except in Cases of Impeachment. He shall have Power, by and with the Advice and Consent of the Senate, to make Treaties, provided two thirds of the Senators present concur; and he shall nominate, and by and with the Advice and Consent of the Senate, shall appoint Ambassadors, other public Ministers and Consuls, Judges of the supreme Court, and all other Officers of the United States, whose Appointments are not herein otherwise provided for, and which shall be established by Law: but the Congress may by Law vest the Appointment of such inferior Officers, as they think proper, in the President alone, in the Courts of Law, or in the Heads of Departments.

The President shall have Power to fill up all Vacancies that may happen during the Recess of the Senate, by granting Commissions which shall expire at the End of their next Session.

Section 3.

He shall from time to time give to the Congress Information of the State of the Union, and recommend to their Consideration such Measures as he shall judge necessary and expedient; he may, on extraordinary

Occasions, convene both Houses, or either of them, and in Case of Disagreement between them, with Respect to the Time of Adjournment, he may adjourn them to such Time as he shall think proper; he shall receive Ambassadors and other public Ministers; he shall take Care that the Laws be faithfully executed, and shall Commission all the Officers of the United States.

Section 4.

The President, Vice President and all civil Officers of the United States, shall be removed from Office on Impeachment for, and Conviction of, Treason, Bribery, or other high Crimes and Misdemeanors.

Article III

A portion of Section 2 was modified by the Eleventh Amendment.

Section 1.

The judicial Power of the United States shall be vested in one supreme Court, and in such inferior Courts as the Congress may from time to time ordain and establish. The Judges, both of the supreme and inferior Courts, shall hold their Offices during good Behaviour, and shall, at stated Times, receive for their Services a Compensation, which shall not be diminished during their Continuance in Office.

Section 2.

The judicial Power shall extend to all Cases, in Law and Equity, arising under this Constitution, the Laws of the United States, and Treaties made, or which shall be made, under their Authority;—to all Cases affecting Ambassadors, other public Ministers and Consuls;—to all Cases of admiralty and maritime Jurisdiction;—to Controversies to which the United States shall be a Party; to Controversies between two or more States;—*between a State and Citizens of another State;*—between Citizens of different States; between Citizens of the same State claiming Lands under Grants of different States, and between a State, or the Citizens thereof, and foreign States, Citizens or Subjects.

In all Cases affecting Ambassadors, other public Ministers and Consuls, and those in which a State shall be Party, the supreme Court shall have original Jurisdiction. In all the other Cases before mentioned, the supreme Court shall have appellate Jurisdiction, both as to Law and

Fact, with such Exceptions, and under such Regulations as the Congress shall make.

The Trial of all Crimes, except in Cases of Impeachment, shall be by Jury; and such Trial shall be held in the State where the said Crimes shall have been committed; but when not committed within any State, the Trial shall be at such Place or Places as the Congress may by Law have directed.

Section 3.

Treason against the United States, shall consist only in levying War against them, or in adhering to their Enemies, giving them Aid and Comfort. No Person shall be convicted of Treason unless on the Testimony of two Witnesses to the same overt Act, or on Confession in open Court.

The Congress shall have Power to declare the Punishment of Treason, but no Attainder of Treason shall work Corruption of Blood, or Forfeiture except during the Life of the Person attainted.

Article IV

A portion of Section 2 was superseded by the Thirteenth Amendment.

Section 1.

Full Faith and Credit shall be given in each State to the public Acts, Records, and judicial Proceedings of every other State. And the Congress may by general Laws prescribe the Manner in which such Acts, Records and Proceedings shall be proved, and the Effect thereof.

Section 2.

The Citizens of each State shall be entitled to all Privileges and Immunities of Citizens in the several States.

A Person charged in any State with Treason, Felony, or other Crime, who shall flee from Justice, and be found in another State, shall on Demand of the executive Authority of the State from which he fled, be delivered up, to be removed to the State having Jurisdiction of the Crime.

No Person held to Service or Labour in one State, under the Laws thereof, escaping into another, shall, in Consequence of any Law or Regulation therein, be discharged from such Service or Labour, but shall be delivered up on Claim of the Party to whom such Service or Labour may be due.

Constitution
of the United
States of
America

Section 3.

New States may be admitted by the Congress into this Union; but no new State shall be formed or erected within the Jurisdiction of any other State; nor any State be formed by the Junction of two or more States, or Parts of States, without the Consent of the Legislatures of the States concerned as well as of the Congress.

The Congress shall have Power to dispose of and make all needful Rules and Regulations respecting the Territory or other Property belonging to the United States; and nothing in this Constitution shall be so construed as to Prejudice any Claims of the United States, or of any particular State.

Section 4.

The United States shall guarantee to every State in this Union a Republican Form of Government, and shall protect each of them against Invasion; and on Application of the Legislature, or of the Executive (when the Legislature cannot be convened), against domestic Violence.

Article V

The Congress, whenever two thirds of both Houses shall deem it necessary, shall propose Amendments to this Constitution, or, on the Application of the Legislatures of two thirds of the several States, shall call a Convention for proposing Amendments, which, in either Case, shall be valid to all Intents and Purposes, as Part of this Constitution, when ratified by the Legislatures of three fourths of the several States, or by Conventions in three fourths thereof, as the one or the other Mode of Ratification may be proposed by the Congress; Provided that no Amendment which may be made prior to the Year One thousand eight hundred and eight shall in any Manner affect the first and fourth Clauses in the Ninth Section of the first Article; and that no State, without its Consent, shall be deprived of its equal Suffrage in the Senate.

Article VI

All Debts contracted and Engagements entered into, before the Adoption of this Constitution, shall be as valid against the United States under this Constitution, as under the Confederation.

This Constitution, and the Laws of the United States which shall be made in Pursuance thereof; and all Treaties made, or which shall be made, under the Authority of the United States, shall be the supreme Law of the Land; and the Judges in every State shall be bound thereby, any Thing in the Constitution or Laws of any State to the Contrary notwithstanding.

The Senators and Representatives before mentioned, and the Members of the several State Legislatures, and all executive and judicial Officers, both of the United States and of the several States, shall be bound by Oath or Affirmation, to support this Constitution; but no religious Test shall ever be required as a Qualification to any Office or public Trust under the United States.

Article VII

The Ratification of the Conventions of nine States, shall be sufficient for the Establishment of this Constitution between the States so ratifying the Same.

Attest William Jackson Secretary

Done in Convention by the Unanimous Consent of the States present the Seventeenth Day of September in the Year of our Lord one thousand seven hundred and Eighty seven and of the Independence of the United States of America the Twelfth In witness whereof We have hereunto subscribed our Names,

G° Washington Presidt and deputy from Virginia

Delaware: Geo: Read, Gunning Bedford jun, John Dickinson, Richard Bassett, Jaco: Broom

Maryland: James McHenry, Dan of St Thos. Jenifer, Danl. Carroll

Virginia: John Blair—, James Madison Jr.

North Carolina: Wm. Blount, Richd. Dobbs Spaight, Hu Williamson

South Carolina: J. Rutledge, Charles Cotesworth Pinckney, Charles Pinckney, Pierce Butler

Georgia: William Few, Abr Baldwin

New Hampshire: John Langdon, Nicholas Gilman

Massachusetts: Nathaniel Gorham, Rufus King

Connecticut: Wm. Saml. Johnson Roger Sherman

New York: Alexander Hamilton

Constitution of the United States of America

New Jersey: Wil: Livingston, David Brearley, Wm. Paterson, Jona: Dayton

Pennsylvania: B Franklin, Thomas Mifflin, Robt. Morris, Geo. Clymer, Thos. FitzSimons, Jared Ingersoll, James Wilson, Gouv Morris

Index

A

Abington School District v. Schempp (1963), 1:7

abortion legislation. *See* amendment proposals and *Roe v. Wade*

Adair v. United States (1908), 1:111

Adams, John, 1:13, 57, 2:224–26, 2:237 (illus.), 2:237–39, 242, 244, 3:393, 438, 466

Adams, John Quincy, 2:243–44, 341

Adams, Samuel, 1:58

Adams v. New York (1904), 1:81–2

Adderly v. Florida (1966), 1:27

Afroyim v. Rusk (1967), 2:278

Age Discrimination in Employment Act of 1967 (ADEA), 1:152

Agostini v. Felton (1997), 1:9

Aguilar v. Felton (1985), 1:9

Aguilar v. Texas (1964), 1:77

Alien and Sedition Acts of 1798, 1:13

Allgeyer v. Louisiana (1897), 1:111, 2:281

amendment proposals, 3:508–28
 abortion, 3:521, 525, 3:525 (illus.)
 balanced budget proposal, 3:514–15, 521
 child labor proposal, 3:513–17, 3:513 (illus.), 3:521
 congressional term limits, 3:521, 525–26
 District of Columbia statehood, 3:447, 522–23

Electoral College reform, 3:521–24
 Equal Rights Amendment (ERA), 3:383, 517–21, 3:517 (illus.)
 flag desecration, 3:521, 524
 nobility proposal, 3:509–11, 3:510 (illus.)

American Medical Association (AMA), 2:189

American Woman Suffrage Association (AWSA), 3:373–74, 376

Anthony, Susan B., 3:373 (illus.), 3:373, 375, 378, 382

Anti–Saloon League, 3:360, 362, 402

Apodaca v. Oregon (1972), 1:127

Apportionment Clause, The, 2:274, 296–97, 298

Arizona v. Evans (1995), 1:86

Arthur, Chester A., 3:468–69

Articles of Confederation, 1:3, 34, 61–2, 74, 92, 121, 145, 162–63, 2:182, 184, 198, 205, 223, 276, 338, 3:422, 437, 498

Ashcraft v. Tennessee, (1944), 1:105

Ashwander v. Tennessee Valley Authority (1936), 2:186

Association Against the Prohibition Amendment (AAPA), 3:409, 412–13

Atlas Roofing Co. v. Occupational Safety & Health Review Commission (1977), 1:155

Attucks, Crispus, 1:58–9, 1:57 (illus.)

Index

Index

Index

Index

Index

Index

Index

Index